THE SOCIAL EUROPE WE NEED

European Social Forum

The Social Europe We Need

By
Robin Blackburn
André Brie MEP
Ken Coates
Christina Beatty & Stephen Fothergill

SPOKESMAN
for
SOCIALIST RENEWAL

First published in 2004 by
Spokesman
Russell House, Bulwell Lane
Nottingham
NG6 0BT
Phone 0115 9708381 Fax 0115 9420433
e-mail elfeuro@compuserve.com
www.spokesmanbooks.com

ISBN 0 85124 703 2

A CIP Catalogue is available from the British Libruary.

Printed by the Russell Press Ltd., (phone 0115 9784505)

Contents

Chapter One

Another Europe Is Possible

Ken Coates

Ken Coates was a Member of the European Parliament for ten years to 1999, and is co-author of The Making of the Labour Movement: The Formation of the Transport & General Workers' Union.

The European Social Forum was inspired by the World Social Forum in Porto Alegre. This defined itself in distinction from the World Economic Forum at Davos, which took on its shoulders all the sins of neo-liberalism with the globalisation of greed. An impressive list of participants has been assembled from non-governmental organisations in a wide variety of countries. Now the European Social Forum will come to London, at the invitation of a number of activist groupings, with the support of London Mayor, Ken Livingstone. We are bound to wish it well, because there is a great vacuum where consequent political discussion used to take place, and there are many urgent social issues about which informed people need to share their experiences. It remains to be seen how widely the Social Forum will be able to cast its net, when it comes to England.

In several European countries at the same time, there are a number of key problems which would clearly benefit from joint analysis, and if it could be achieved, common action.

It is not difficult to see why the European Social Forums have established a prototype for this kind of convergence. Basing themselves on the traditions, and the Charter of Principles agreed by the World Social Forum, which met in Porto Alegre, Brazil, the European Social Forum met first of all in Florence, and then, last year, in Paris. Each gathering attracted tens of thousands of participants, from a very wide variety of social movements, non-governmental organisations and trade unions.

The slogan of the World Social Forum, 'Another World is Possible', touched a vein of idealism and commitment which fired many young people to identify with it. It stood out in clear contrast to the compromised behaviour of so many established institutions in Europe, including, unhappy to say, many governments and established political parties. The World Social Forum made clear its opposition to 'the process of globalisation commanded by the large multinational corporations and by the governments and international institutions (which are) at the service of these corporations' interests'. It was able to draw on the practical experiences of non-governmental organisations and aid organisations, as well as movements in defence of the environment and community organisations with a wide variety of aims.

The World Social Forum found itself confronting a global power structure: but it did not retreat into parochialism, seeking instead to find the way to an alternative world. Just as it was finding new bases for coherence, the rising tide of militarism engulfed the world in new conflicts, culminating in the dreadful invasion of Iraq, in which Iraqi sources have identified thirty-seven thousand civilian deaths. (The Blitz of the Luftwaffe in England killed twenty-two thousand people.)

So it was that this continuing international discussion reached out from engaging with myriad social problems to embracing the growing world-wide peace movement. A predominant element of spontaneity governed this process, which represented a coming together of many tributaries, innumerable initiatives, and centres of goodwill.

In Britain, a political crisis which had already shown itself in numerous other European countries was becoming evident and acute. For decades, dissent in all its forms, and pressures of innumerable reforms, had found their focus in the Labour Party. Of course, not every critic of the established society could join that Party, but all were likely to find their behaviour influenced by it. But openness to all the schools of rebellion became identified with sterile oppositionism, and a new generation of political leaders arose which sought out and established a new conformity, based upon manipulation and media consent, and ruthless accommodation to the established powers. Assiduous courtship of the Murdoch news empire was but a token of the engagement of this new political establishment. No wonder it became important for any idealist, and all those alien to cynicism, to insist that 'another world is possible'. Legions of non-governmental activists, trade union members, Church militants and other volunteers found the prevailing official climate of public organisations increasingly oppressive. Even when good actions were performed by government, they were usually overlaid with spin and wider deception.

That is why, in England, there is a great deal of space for the European Social Forum, if it can maintain its ready traditions of openness and engagement with the important issues which continue to trouble our society.

One of these is clearly mass unemployment. In England, followers of the official statistics believe that this problem has been solved. But scholars who are willing to dig deeper, think not. Christina Beatty and Stephen Fothergill have looked in depth at the numbers of long-term sickness claimants, many of whom, for a considerable time, have been refugees from the provision for unemployment relief (see chapter 5). They have concluded that, in parts of England, in the North, as well as in Scotland and Wales, there are some two and a half million unemployed people, who depend on sickness related benefits to keep body and soul together, although in fact there are no jobs for them. The employment position in England has eased in recent years, but this level of hardship remains quite unacceptable.

When I was in the European Parliament, I drew on the earlier calculations of Stephen Fothergill and his colleagues in the course of preparing two pan-European Conventions of unemployed people, which met in the Parliament building in Brussels, and enabled the unemployed and sympathetic scholars and activists to compare notes and co-ordinate their efforts for the recovery of jobs. These Conventions drew support from all the main political Groups in the European Parliament, although they were initiated by members of the Socialist, Green and United Left Groups. Three of the most energetic activists in the European Parliament, who supported these initiatives, are no longer Members. But there are very many reasons why a forum of the unemployed is necessary, and indeed has become more necessary than it was, as the problem of unemployment has worsened in a number of countries, and gone underground in others.

These initiatives were part of a broader attempt to bring together groupings within civil society, in order to reinforce political attempts to deal with problems. My first initiative in this respect was the Pensioners' Parliament, which the European Parliament's Socialist Group agreed to promote, and which brought together five hundred-plus pensioners from every country in the European Union, to seek to compare provision and experiences between one country and another, and to try to agree on common goals. This meeting was deemed to have been very successful, so much so that it was repeated the following year as a joint initiative of all the Groups in the European Parliament.

I was very pleased when, quite spontaneously, a group of disabled people came to the European Parliament to ask for hospitality for a parliament of European disabled people. At first, many of the Parliament's officials were very sceptical about this request, but a powerful lobby among the handicapped, the blind, the deaf, and the victims of a wide range of disabilities, after a lobby of the wheelchairs and white sticks, won the agreement of a majority of Members of the Parliament, and the Disabled People's Parliament duly met in the newly opened hemicycle in Brussels. I was asked to give a brief opening speech, where I learnt the meaning of a prolonged session of waving by members of the audience. This, I was informed, was deaf people's applause.

The idea of the Social Forums is wider, and potentially more creative, since it can bring together people from an immense diversity of organisations, NGOs and specialist groups, and help to empower them by enriching the field of their contacts.

Previous efforts to develop wider associations of NGOs in practical collaboration tended to find their focus in the existing political organisations. But today it is a mark of gathering social crisis that worse problems are accompanied by fewer official openings for redress. Old social democracies sought to manage change in society. Now, with some skill, they seek to understand and to manage change in the reporting of society, and the systematic manipulation and under-weighting of its bad news. Thus we get a flow of tainted information, misleading statistics, fabricated intelligence. Today we have the age of the official lie. That is why inclusive and comprehensive meetings are so valuable, and should certainly be continued and developed.

But the experience of our people insists that another world is really possible, and invites us to move beyond our general forum, towards more specific and conventional meetings of minds, tracing out the lineaments of that other practice which will bring the other world into fruition.

Chapter Two

The Europe We Need

Robin Blackburn

Robin Blackburn is an editor of New Left Review and the author of Banking on Death, or Investing in Life: the History and Future of Pensions, *published by Verso. He teaches in the Sociology Department at the University of Essex and can be reached on roblack@essex.ac.uk*

Europe today faces three shocks which threaten its social institutions and aspiration for an independent role in world affairs. They are the shock of rampant United States power, the shock of Anglo-Saxon economics, and the shock of a poorly planned European Union enlargement. While these processes have a long-term character, they now possess enough concentrated force to paralyse European institutions, and to subject the continent to corporate-led globalisation domestically and to United States 'leadership', as the White House now calls its imperial role in global affairs. This is not the Europe the world – or its own citizens – needs.

Because the European Union is, at present, the only global entity with an economic weight and political potential equal to that of the United States, it has – in principle – the best possibility of defying the new hegemon. This should not at all be a question of making Europe more like the United States – a process which has already gone too far – but, instead, of ensuring that Europe represents a different social model and that on the international stage it refuses to chain itself to the chariot wheels of the Bush regime.

Europe's leaders trail behind the United States

Europe has an opportunity for a creative response to the challenges it faces. This is partly because US leadership is itself in deep difficulties, above all in Iraq and the Middle East. And it is also because the sterile formula of Europe's own grotesquely-named 'growth and stability' pact has been breached by the European Union's two leading core states. This represents a break with the baneful rule of the European Central Bank and its disastrous monetarist dogmas.

Europe's response to the impasse of US strategy in Iraq, and to the crisis of European Union monetary governance, does not measure up to the opportunity presented. Rather, it weakens Europe and betrays the hopes of peoples around the world who would like to see some check on US power.

The Nato allies protest publicly or privately about US 'unilateralism', but then proceed to endorse its consequences. The main Nato powers voted in the United Nations to give the US occupation and its plans a quite unwarranted post-facto legitimacy. As the United States gets into deeper trouble it will again expect its meeker allies to send more troops; that is to put their own citizens in harm's way, in order temporarily to contain a dangerous situation. George W. Bush and Colin Powell are already pursuing this policy, but John Kerry claims that he would have greater success.

At home, the rule of the European Central Bank will be rescued and recycled by giving even greater scope to explicit and 'implicit' privatisation. The latter is the process whereby public services and social protections are degraded in order to oblige the mass of citizens to buy social protection from rapacious finance and insurance houses. Blair, Rafarin, Schröder and Berlusconi have all been pursuing such commodification of social insurance and educational provision. Each have curbed pension provision, and created new opportunities for the financial services industry. However, the latter are looking for more generous tax relief for those who buy their products, a tax subsidy that would absorb much of their costly marketing. The next charge of the 'reformers' will be led by Nicholas Sarkozy, the French finance minister, and José Manuel Barroso, the newly appointed president of the European Commission.

The new course has encountered large-scale, but episodic, resistance: the peace demonstrations of 15 February 2003, strikes and demonstrations against pension cutbacks, opposition to student fees, the rejection of the government in the French local elections, the defeat of Aznar in Spain, and the drubbing administered to New Labour and most other ruling parties in the European elections in June 2004. Continuing attacks on education and welfare will create excellent opportunities to challenge the misleaders of Europe, and to open up conflicts and fissures in the 'grand coalition' of Schröder and

Raffarin, Chirac and Sarkozy, Berlusconi and Blair. The disarray of the ruling parties furnishes an opportunity to spell out the core elements of an alternative to neo-liberal Europe.

But whether at home or abroad this alternative must break openly and clearly with what has gone before. In Spain, Zapatero, the Socialist leader, won because he had strongly opposed Spanish backing for the US invasion and occupation of Iraq. Europe's leaders have yet to register the political defeat that the occupiers have already suffered. There is only one way that a future Iraqi government could acquire legitimacy and that is to insist on the complete evacuation of occupation troops, the return of Iraqi oil and the cancellation of the decrees and acts of the occupation authority. If Europe backed the evacuation of the occupying forces, this would not only offer the chance for a new start in Iraq but would chime in with the hopes of tens of millions of Americans.

Europe's leaders also refuse to face the reality that the US economic model, far from being worthy of emulation, is today mired in failure. The collapse of Enron was just the beginning of a rash of scandals which involve every leading financial institution on Wall Street. Over the last two years, Eliot Spitzer, the New York attorney general, has brought forward investigations and charges which show the large US banks and 'mutual funds' to have been allowing hedge funds to 'skim' (rob) the pension accounts of over ninety million savers. This was the consequence of de-regulation and 'financialisation'. It is accompanied by extravagant returns to chief executives and financial intermediaries, and heavy erosion of pension fund assets.

As 'Anglo-Saxon' economics advance in Europe, it has similar effects – without, so far, an Eliot Spitzer to expose their full scope. Europe now has its own string of corporate scandals – Parmalat, Shell, Vivendi, Ahold and others. These testify to the corroding effect of financial engineering and show how the latest ingenious products of the international banks and accounting firms can give new scope to age-old European traditions of élite corruption. Pension funds have been hit and many have seen their savings shrink. While new scope is given to the commercial banks and insurance houses, social gains such as the 35 hour week are being driven back by employers who can threaten re-location. Meanwhile, as the *Wall Street Journal* headline puts it 'European CEO Pay is Taking Off'.[1]

Anglo-American corporate welfare destroys good jobs

The US recession of 2000-3 destroyed two and a half million 'good' jobs, and the current weak recovery has seen few of those jobs replaced. The US public rightly worries that the regime of commercial social insurance, which excludes a fifth or more of the population, will fail even most of those it does cover over the next decade or two. Private pensions and health care suffer from a severe 'cost disease'. Competitive marketing consumes vast amounts of money while 'customising' provision for each individual is costly and cumbersome. The loss of manufacturing jobs is also rooted in the problems of large manufacturing concerns which now have large pension fund deficits (in the US these now total $350 billion, in the UK £65 billion).

Many on the US left look to Europe for an alternative, but are increasingly disappointed when they do so. It is true that social protection remains far better in Europe. But even governments of the Left – like that of the Social Democrats and Greens in Germany – lacking the courage and imagination to find better ways to finance welfare, cut benefits instead. This is what Prodi's centre-left government in Italy did in the late 1990s and what he will do again if he ousts Berlusconi.

It is understandable that governments of the Left decline further to raise the already heavy taxes on employment. These taxes are generally not 'progressive'. They fall heavily on workers earning only average or low salaries. Laying a 'tax wedge' of 40 per cent on average incomes, they consequently weaken demand and discourage high rates of employment. With officially-recognised unemployment running at 10 per cent, and many of the unemployed not even getting on the register, certain categories of the population – above all the under-25s and the over-50s – have been condemned to poverty and idleness. Not surprisingly, the demagogues of the far right have often flourished in these conditions.

If we compare the Anglo-Saxon economies with Europe we find that they generate different types of unemployment. Europe's high 'payroll taxes' weaken demand and deter the creation of formal jobs in the service sector, helping to explain why employment rates amongst the proportion of the population aged 18-65 are ten to fifteen percentage points lower than in the United States or the United Kingdom.[2]

But the 'Anglo-Saxon' tradition of encouraging corporations to furnish tax-subsidised pension and health benefits has had a devastating impact on manufacturing employment. Many famous Anglo-American corporations find it impossible to maintain healthy levels of investment and employment because they are weighed down by pension and health deficits. Companies such as Ford, Boeing, American Airlines, US Steel, Goodyear, Maytag, Colgate-Palmolive, Unilever, BT, Rolls Royce and GKN have deficits in their pension funds worth more than half the value of the corporation itself. They are forced to divert huge sums of money to remedy those deficits and to fire thousands of employees.

The Anglo-American corporate welfare schemes are 'pro-cyclical'. That is to say that, during good times, the employers can take a 'contribution holiday' because the value of the shares in the fund rises. British corporations skipped £28 billion of pension fund contributions between 1988 and 2000, which is part of the reason that they are in deep deficit today. In bad times, when it is most difficult, the sponsoring corporation has to stump up cash, because the value of shares in the fund has dropped. The better designed European corporate schemes at least require companies to put away more as special 'reserves' in good times, when it is easier to do so. But all types of corporate-sponsored welfare have the drawback that they are linked to one company, which may itself fail, leaving employees with depleted benefits. In July, the collapse of Federal Mogul, a car parts supplier, halved the pension benefit of 20,000 British workers and cut the expected benefit of a further 20,000 in an associated company.

The pension fund promises that companies make are legally enforceable. This means they take precedence over current investment and current employees. The structure of corporate welfare encourages, or even obliges, companies in difficulties to rob Peter to pay Paul – or rather to sack Peter to pay Paul. The need to bale out pension funds has destroyed hundreds of thousands of jobs in high-end manufacturing in the United States. Likewise in the United Kingdom, manufacturing has been losing 5,000 jobs a week, but Gordon Brown, the Labour Chancellor, has maintained the overall employment level by creating more than half a million jobs in the public sector. (Also note that the real extent of UK unemployment is concealed by the fact that 2.3 million receive 'incapacity benefit', a figure four times as great as 20 years ago.) The end result is that, despite all the weakness of the continental European economy, its exports and manufacturing corporations are stronger than those of the United Kingdom and the United States.

It should be clear that Europe needs a better way of paying for proper old age and health protection than it has – but also a better one than the Anglo-American paths of individualisation or corporate welfare. We need to find other ways to finance the social programmes we need. There are still many positive features of the European social model. Working hours are short, but productivity is high. Decent health care is more widely available than in the United Kingdom, let alone the United States, with its inflated commercial charges. Europe's often beautiful countryside, its many handsome towns and cities, and the successful rehabilitation of several formerly-blighted industrial zones, all testify that a sense of the integrity of public space has not yet been entirely lost.

But the best way to defend what is good in the European social model is to go on the offensive, elaborating a new political economy, one capable of finding needed resources to underwrite social programmes, and of reigning in, and ultimately controlling, the forces of financialisation.

The share levy: a new way to finance future social spending

It is now some time since governments of the Left dared to ask whether the owners of the large corporations might be obliged to contribute more to the wider society, without which their own profits would be impossible. The most far-seeing attempt to think through the types of new finance that would be needed to guarantee generous social provision was Rudolf Meidner's advocacy of 'wage-earner funds' in the 1970s and 1980s.

Rudolf Meidner was – together with Gosta Rehn – the architect of the Swedish welfare state. He was Chief Economist of the LO, Sweden's main trade union federation. He produced an impressive body of policy-oriented economic analysis that deserved – and still deserves – to win the Nobel Prize. A distinguishing feature of his approach was that the working of social funds was harmonised with both a wage-bargaining round and the protection of high employment levels.

Anticipating the new social expenditures that would be entailed by an ageing and learning society he argued for the setting up of strategic social funds to be financed by a share levy. This did not work like traditional corporate taxation, which subtracts from cash-flow and, potentially, investment. Instead Meidner's levy falls on wealthy shareholders, the value of whose holdings is diluted, not on the resources of the corporation as a productive concern. According to the original plan every company with more than fifty employees was obliged to issue new shares every year equivalent to 20 per cent of its profits. The newly issued shares – which could not be sold for several years – were to be given to a network of 'wage earner funds', representing trade unions and local authorities. The latter would hold the shares, and reinvest the income they yielded from dividends, in order to finance future social expenditure. As the wage earner funds grew they would be able to play an increasing part in directing policy in the corporations which they owned.[3]

Meidner's visionary scheme was strongly supported by trade unions and the members of the Social Democratic party, but strongly opposed by the privately owned media, and by the 'twenty families' who dominate the country's large corporations. After a scare campaign the Social Democratic government eventually withdrew the proposed share levy but set up social funds financed by a profits tax. These were wound up by the incoming Conservatives in 1992. So Meidner's plan has yet to be tried.

The need for a new layer of European social provision

The visible crumbling of Europe's ability to protect its own citizens weakens its voice in world affairs. A determined effort to rescue its collapsing social model could be achieved if the Union itself sponsored at least some new social provision for all citizens. Interestingly enough, this was the approach of President Franklin Roosevelt in the 1930s when the United States faced its own most serious social crisis. The Social Security Act of 1935 became the so-called 'third rail' of US politics. Eventually it covered everyone and the Social Security card became a badge of civic identity.

US Social Security redistributed from rich to poor – including from rich regions to poor ones – in ways that promoted a minimum of national unity. The European Union today has no social programmes. The best it has are so-called 'convergence' funds, the Common Agricultural Policy and schemes targeted at new members. But these do not cover everybody, as does Social Security, and have much less resources than the US programme. While the Common Agricultural Policy has a budget of 50 billion euros each year – roughly $45 billion – US Social Security has a budget of nearly $400 billion annually to pay old age and disability pensions for forty million US citizens.

Of course, US Social Security is far less generous than most European equivalents, and is today threatened with privatisation by President Bush. Nevertheless it does help to bind together the citizens of the different states and to help focus loyalty to the political order.

Three economists – James Galbraith, Pedro Conceicao and Pedro Ferreira – have argued for a 'truly European welfare state, with a continental retirement programme' and 'the creation of major new universities of the first water...in the beautiful, lower income regions of the European periphery and the full funding of students to attend them.'[4]

A Europe-wide welfare regime could also encourage better child-care provision. The problem of the ageing society is as much the result of a low birth rate as it is of increased longevity. It is striking that today Scandinavia, with its generous attention to child care, has a much higher birth rate than Mediterranean Europe. It is also interesting that the introduction of the 35 hour week in France coincided with a small but significant recovery in the French birth rate. Improvements to social welfare, education and working conditions should be pursued for their own sake, but they will often contribute to a broader social framework of well-being.

A European-wide welfare regime should be organised on a universal basis so that every citizen and every country receives some benefit. Special supplements might be available on a regional basis so that poorer regions in the wealthier states would also benefit.

If a European Union-wide Meidner-style corporate levy – set initially at ten per cent of corporate profits – was introduced, the resources raised could be put in the hands of regional networks of democratically-administered social funds. This should be conceived of as an addition to – not a replacement of – national welfare policies which, where necessary, might also be able to draw on emergency help from the Europe-wide fund. Levied on a continent-wide basis, the arrangements would contribute towards 'tax harmonisation' and help to deter social dumping. The new member states have low corporate taxes – Estonia's are to be zero on reinvested profits – while their income taxes are broadly similar to those in many parts of Western Europe. Under a share levy scheme wherever corporations were located they would have to issue new shares to the social funds based on their profits anywhere in Europe. Two-thirds of the yield would be distributed to the fund network inside each member country and one-third would be distributed on a continent-wide basis in proportion to population. So the social funds located in new member states would benefit from a central as well as local distribution. This would not only help them to raise expenditure on social and educational purposes but also give their local funds greater leverage, as institutional shareholders, over the multinational corporations.

It might be objected that if the powerful Swedish Social Democrats and trade unions were defeated when they tried to introduce such a measure, why is there any reason to think that something similar could be achieved in the new Europe where labour is now much weaker? My answer would be that there are four reasons why the outcome could be different. Firstly, European corporations are not as tightly organised and cohesive as Sweden's twenty families. Secondly, recent social mobilisations in Europe have been stronger and more persistent on pensions than any other issue. Thirdly, ruling parties have proved to be exceptionally vulnerable when they try to weaken and undermine social provision. Fourthly, it would be possible to frame the social fund proposals in ways that anticipate the sort of opposition that blocked advance in Sweden.

The share levy at ten per cent of profits would have the effect of diluting the value of all shares by about one per cent. Contrary to myth, individual share-holding is still confined to a small minority in

Europe. Nevertheless bona fide pension funds also hold shares and it might be claimed that they would lose out. Most would be likely to gain more than they lost by the levy – if there was any doubt about this, they could be directly compensated by an allocation from the social funds.

The ownership of shares is still very unequal so the levy would work like a wealth tax. Unlike other attempts to tax wealth the share levy would not fall on home ownership or small farms and businesses – to meet this problem wealth taxes invariably allow exemptions which turn into handy loop-holes and reduce the value of the revenue they raise. Other revenue sources which could be tapped to boost social and educational expenditure would be a tax on increases in the value of commercial land and a tax on fossil fuels. Together these levies and taxes would ensure that corporations would help to finance the social fabric on which their operations entirely depend and to give all citizens a share in the fruits of economic advance.

The European Trade Union Confederation has long called for the setting up of a proper, continent-wide Social Fund, with resources which it could invest to generate productive employment and that could underwrite future welfare expenditure. In 1959, the then European Community established a European Investment Bank, which was meant to counter-balance the power of the central banks. With the scrapping of the 'growth and stability pact' there is more than ever a role for the European Investment Bank. Indeed, three Cambridge economists have argued that the European Investment Bank should be built up as a counter-weight to the European Central Bank.[5]

The social funds would also be as much about producing wealth as distributing it. In a continent where stock exchanges are already of greatly increased importance, the social funds could help to protect productive enterprises from 'financialisation', to promote socially responsible business objectives, and to assert a degree of popular control over the accumulation process. The network of pension funds would have significant power in corporate affairs, both because of their shares and their investment policies. The fund network would develop its own cadre of financial specialists and would have reason to assist the tax authorities to monitor and enforce fiscal regulations.[6]

But, it might be objected, is not a fund based on shares vulnerable to the inevitable swings of the market? Dividend income is, in fact, much less volatile than share price, and the networks would count on dividends not share sales for their income. The pension fund network would be encouraged to use dividend revenue to buy corporate and public bonds to diversify their holdings. The network would also have to offer unquoted private companies the option of contributing bonds rather than shares. The networks would be barred from selling the shares they hold – Meidner's approach to social provision is to follow the method of 'de-commodification', in this case means of production. The social fund would, in the first instance, concentrate on building up resources for the future to pay for the sharp increase in social expenditure that will be required by two fundamental processes – the ageing of the population and the increasing need for further education and lifelong learning.

In the end, of course, the social expenditure of the future will have to be paid out of the production of the future, and this means that some future incomes will have to be allocated to this purpose. The share levy approach ensures that *rentier* incomes – returns to capital – will be diverted from wealthy individuals to the network of social funds.

Europe would, of course, be better able to dedicate itself to saving and improving its welfare arrangements and educational provision if it does not allow itself to be dragged into US military exploits. Washington's bellicosity is itself prompted by the desire to distract US citizens from grave social problems, and ballooning inequality, at home. Europe should aspire to a quite different model, both for its own people and in its relations with the rest of the world. Developing some welfare ties at a continental level, binding together old and new members, would help to build the sense of common citizenship which might underpin an independent and progressive foreign policy.

Notes

1 *Wall Steet Journal*, 23 July, 2004.

2 Robin Blackburn, 'Eurodenial', *New Left Review*, No 18, November-December 2003; see also Andrea Boltho, 'What's Wrong with Europe?', *New Left Review*, No 22, July-August 2003

3 The original plan is set out in Rudolf Meidner, *Employee Investment Funds*,

London 1978. For an account of the struggles over its implementation see Jonas Pontusson, 'Sweden: the People's Home in Danger', in Perry Anderson and Patrick Camiller, eds. *Mapping the Left In Western Europe*, London 1994.

4 James K. Galbraith, Pedro Conceicao and Pedro Ferreira, 'Inequality and Unemployment in Europe', *New Left Review*, Sept-Oct 1999.

5 Philip Arestis, Kevin McCauley and Malcolm Sawyer, 'An Alternative Stability Pact for the European Union, *Cambridge Journal of Economics*, vol 25, no 1, 2001.

6 Though multinationals have many ways of evading tax through the use of transfer pricing, and the manipulation of allowances, the fiscal authorities, if properly supported by legislators, are far from powerless. For example, they can combat the siphoning off of profits as interest on intra-group loans – 'thin capitalisation' – by using operating profit as the basis for their calculations. See the interesting – if over-optimistic – report by Michael P. Devereux, Rachel Griffith, and Alexander Klemm, 'Why Has the UK Corporation Tax Raised So much Revenue?', Institute of Fiscal Studies, London, February 2004. I look at other technical aspects of 'Meidner-style' levies, including the likely yield, in 'The Pension Gap and How to Fix It', *Challenge*, September-October 2004 and 'How to Rescue a Failing Pension System: the British Case', in *New Political Economy*, December 2004.

Chapter Three

Social Policy in Europe

The Demolition of the Social State

André Brie MEP

The author is a well-known member of the European Parliament who represents the Party of Democratic Socialism in Germany.

The shattered dream of unified, social Europe

The common experience of resistance against the regimes of Hitler and Mussolini and the occupation policies of the 'axis powers' during World War II led to debates within the broad anti-fascist spectrum concerning the necessity to unify Europe. From diverse national groups there emerged a European movement, which after the end of the Second World War experienced a brief idealistic blossoming. For this movement, the creation of a *social Europe* after overcoming fascism and war stood at the top of the agenda. It consciously advocated a European perspective (*United States of Europe*) for reconstructing democracy, which was to be nourished from the different traditions of anti-fascist resistance.

Thus the 'Manifesto of Ventotene', inspired by Altiero Spinelli and his fellows in what became the socio-libertarian Italian *Partito d'Azione*, as early as 1941 demanded a new ordering of Europe, aimed at a mixed economy and socialisation of the key industries: 'the European revolution has to be socialist in order to do justice to our needs; it must strive for the emancipation of the working class and the creation of more human conditions of life. The needle of this compass, however, should not be pointed in a purely theoretical direction, in which private ownership of the means of production has to be abolished completely or only tolerated temporarily. Private property should be tackled on a case-by-case basis, and either abolished, constrained, corrected or expanded as appears appropriate, and should not be subject to over-simple dogma and moralising. This approach fits in perfectly with the developmental process of a European economic life liberated from the constrictions of militarism and national bureaucracy. Rational solutions ought to replace the irrational, in the outlook of the working people.'

The Manifesto also argued that reconstruction of the European economy should be grounded in the principles of the social state: 'the almost unlimited capacity for mass production of basic goods, thanks to modern technology, today permits everyone to secure, at relatively minor social costs, dwelling, food and clothing, as well as a minimum of comfort indispensable to human dignity. Human solidarity towards those who succumb in the economic struggle, however, should not assume charitable forms which humiliate the recipient and provoke precisely the ills it seeks to combat. We should, on the contrary, adopt a series of measures which enable everyone to enjoy a decent standard of living, whether he or she can work or not, without at the same time lowering the incentive to work and to save. Thus people will no longer be forced to accept oppressive working conditions out of desperation.'

The Hertensteiner programme of the German *Europaunion* of 1946, similarly called for a federated, united and social Europe: 'the European Union cares for the planned reconstruction and economic, social and cultural cooperation as well as for the employment of technical progress exclusively at the service of humanity. The European Community is not directed against anyone and renounces all power politics, and, at the same time, refuses to be the tool of any foreign power.'

This declaration manifested the emerging conflict of the new ordering of Europe with the United States on the one side, and the Soviet Union on the other. But in 1950, when in the newly founded Federal Republic the first enthusiasm was already fading, the German Council of the European Movement demanded a European policy of full employment, of employee mobility and the build-up of a comprehensive system of social protection. It was oriented towards the 'ideal of unified European social insurance and protection law', which would 'provide for all-European reciprocity of benefits and take the necessary steps for clearing and equalising up?' (Mühlbach 1950). The European movements were thus aiming at the step-by-step construction of a European social and welfare state.

With the growing 'systems competition' and the beginning of the

Cold War, the possibilities for European movements to implement their visions in the practical formation of policies declined. The idea of a unified, social Europe as a 'Third Way', in opposition to 'Soviet Communism' and 'US Capitalism', defended by Social Christian, social democratic and trade union circles in the European movement, increasingly lost ground. Eastern Europe, following the notion of 'people's democracy', was firmly tied to the Soviet area of influence. In Western Europe, the USA and the West European political élites linked to it (for example, Adenauer, Schumann, Monnet) certainly pursued an independent European integration project. However, it was aimed functionally only at the creation of a West European market space and the restoration of capitalism. Yet, at the national level, not necessarily the West European level, the West European project was quite certainly linked to the build-up and extension of structures of the social state.

Social policy – the stepchild of European integration

The first 30 years and more of West European integration – from the founding of the three European Communities: European Community for Coal and Steel (ECCS), European Economic Community (EEC) and European Atomic Community (EURATOM) in the 1950s to the single market project in 1986, were marked by an economic and social development model that was widely called the 'Fordist-corporatist welfare state'. The basis for it was the establishment of a 'class compromise' between the labour movement and business at the level of the national state. This on the one hand stabilised a liberal, open market economy. On the other hand, fast economic growth made possible wage increases and the cushioning of social risks by state welfare measures. EC integration in this era largely served as protection for 'Fordist' development paths within the national states. Especially in the early years, they were designed primarily by US-oriented, anti-Communist politicians of the Catholic-conservative camp. At the European level, the development of the market had top priority. Social policy was considered secondary – following the principle of subsidiarity, it was already regulated and strongly anchored at the national level.

I
Social policy in the EEC (1957 – 1974)

The Treaty for the European Community for Coal and Steel of 1951 already contained a few social policy provisions. The formulations and fields for action of the EEC Treaty of 1957 in the area of social policy contained for the most part non-committal declarations of intent. They concentrated mainly upon measures to counteract the existing constraints on mobility of workers and employees in the European Community. The following fields of actions in the area of social policy could be found in the EEC- Treaty:

- equalisation of social insurance systems (Article 51)
- improvement of life and working conditions (Article 117)
- promotion of cooperation in socio-political questions (Article 118)
- social protection of migrant workers (Article 51)
- promotion of professional and geographical mobility with the help of the European Social Fund (Article 123 to 127).

The European Social Fund was established in 1960, and at the beginning financed predominately re-training and re-location measures. Until the mid-1970s, it constituted practically the most important activity of European social policy. In 1970, finally, a European framework for coordinating the social insurance legislation of national states was created and later on developed further. Thereby, it guaranteed that citizens (women and men) of the member countries could move freely within community territory. If they work in another member country, they may not, in the social security arena, be treated worse than the citizens of that country, irrespective of sex. That claims to legally regulated social security can be transferred across internal EC frontiers by migrant workers is in part due to the coordination of the systems of national states (thus pensions, unemployment benefits, health insurance abroad, but not social aid) and claims earned abroad (e.g. pensions) are aggregated according to a unified credit system.

In 1974, the first 'Social Action Programme' of the European Community was implemented. The social policy programmes as a rule relied on general competence norms (Article 100 and 235 ECT) and presupposed unanimous decisions in the Council. The goals of the 'Social Action Programmes' were the protection of full employment, the improvement of life and working conditions within the perspective of their Community-wide equalisation, and the increase in the participation of the social partners in economic and social policy decisions, as well as the working people in the fate of enterprises in the whole EEC. In this respect, however, the question was not of binding declarations of intent corresponding to the then reigning spirit of 'Keynesian global steering'. The main points of emphasis of the more concrete European social policy, since the mid-1970s, were specific action programmes concerning security and health protection in the workplace, the integration of disadvantaged groups into the labour market, rules for coordinating social security for migrant workers, and for the promotion of equality of opportunities for women. European policy of equality of opportunity in fact made a relevant contribution to the rise in consciousness and to partial changes in legislation in the more conservative member states.

Stagnation of European integration ('Eurosclerosis', 1979-1985)
The phase of 'Eurosclerosis' was marked by a general stagnation in the progress of integration and an increasing return to national level of economic policy. Given a background of fundamental changes in the economic conditions of exploitation, in the final analysis, it ended the economic and social developmental model of 'socially embedded, Keynesian-corporatist liberalism'. Above all, the new British government of Margaret Thatcher prevented any kind of progress in the further development of Social Action Programmes and corresponding European legislation. Commission president Jacques Delors in 1984, it is true, managed to push through an initiative to let social partners at the European level enter into a 'social dialogue'. Behind that stood the idea to install a 'social partnership' at the European level, which later on was supposed to usher in a European system of collective agreements. Yet, except for non-binding talks and declarations, nothing ensued. The employers' organisations refused to bargain at the European level. The work and wage policy conflicts increasingly shifted to the level of the firm.

The Domestic market, the Euro and currency union: reorganisation of the pattern of integration
With the Single European Act of 1986/87, there began a far-reaching remodelling of European integration towards a '*competitive-state-based*

integration method'[1]. It is based on an all-European strategy of lowering costs, so as to benefit enterprises and thus promote their international 'competitiveness', as well as removing tasks from the state and 'slimming' it down (liberalisation and privatisation of hitherto state-provided or regulated public services such as energy supply, the railways, post, telecommunications and so on).

The domestic market project was grounded in the principle of regulated competition (mutual recognition of product standards, low harmonisation of corresponding provisions at the European level, competition between the tax and social systems of the national states). Also, as far as the economic and currency union and the Euro-financial regime were concerned, motives of competition and financial policy played the main role. The so-called convergence criteria of the Maastricht Treaty were oriented towards the priority of the fight against inflation, and especially towards the reduction in budget deficits and in the overall levels of national debt. Thus, social expenditures perceived as 'consumption' increasingly came under pressure. Within the currency union, essentially wages are left as the variable that has to adapt, because the possibilities for exchange rate policy are eliminated. The same philosophy is at the core of the creation of an integrated European financial market. The integration pattern based on the competitive state thus constantly puts social provisions in national states under pressure, and increasingly undermines their basis.

In the light of this background, it may at first sight appear paradoxical that in European agreements since 1986, social policy concerns have at least been symbolically restored in a gradual manner. The first phase (1986-1992) distinguished itself by some small steps in this direction. The Single European Act placed great emphasis on the goal of 'social cohesion' (Articles 130 a to e) and tried to sustain it by the extension of the European Structural and Regional Funds. Article 118a introduced the principle of majority decisions in the Council with respect to 'questions of working environment' (in particular health and safety protection at work). Then Commission president Jacques Delors wanted to push through a more comprehensive 'social dimension of the domestic market', but he did not succeed. Article 118 b only enshrined the 'social dialogue' (as a possibility for the participation of employers and trade unions in the 'social design' of the domestic market). The 'Community Charter of Basic Social Rights' adopted by the European Council of Ministers in 1989, (without the United Kingdom, however), entailed no legal obligation and, moreover, continued to hold on to the primary responsibility of the national state for social policy.

Maastricht Treaty and the Founding of the European Union: Social policy without Great Britain

The Maastricht Treaty (Treaty on the Founding of the European Union) of 1991 did not lead to any essential social policy innovations, but to a tricky legal exception. Because Britain refused any integration of social policy concerns at the contractual level, the remaining eleven member states passed the so-called social protocol as well as the Maastricht Treaty on Social Policy. It determined for these eleven member states social policy questions which might fall under common regulatory competence:

- minimal standards for work conditions (which may be adopted by qualified majority),
- social security, protection against dismissal, and information and consultation rights of working people (by unanimous vote),
- social dialogue of the social partners, which allows 'contractual relations including the conclusion of agreements' at the European level.

Thus in the 1990s, various new European guidelines arrived, together with modifications of old ones, which in some areas anchored minimum social standards in the domestic market concerning:

- health and safety at work (machinery guidelines, work protection in the construction of scaffolding, computer screen work guidelines, and so on),
- general conditions of employment (maximum working time as well as holidays, night and shift work, atypical working, employee dismissal, work relationships codified in writing),
- equality of opportunity for women (equality of wages, general equal treatment, burden of proof),
- crises of firms (mergers and takeovers, mass redundancies, insolvency),
- work protection of pregnant women and young people at work,
- participation of workers and employees (guideline about European

Work Councils, information and consultation of working people). The European Social Funds (ESF) were given a wider remit. In the 1980s, they had been employed primarily to tackle the problem of unemployed youth. A majority of funds had been channelled to the poorer member states. The 'Delors Packages' (1988 and 1992) increased and extended the application of the Structural Funds. In this framework, the European Social Funds took on tasks primarily in the area of the struggle against long-term unemployment, the integration of youth into working life, the adaptation of the workforce to industrial structural change, and accompanying measures for the renewal of traditional industrial regions.

The extended social dialogue made it possible for the two European employers' federations and the European Trade Union Confederation, as already mentioned, to pass common declarations or to reach agreements on certain topics. Negotiated agreements between the European social partners could, upon a proposal by the Commission, be converted by the Council into a European guideline. This happened, for example with the European Union Agreement of the Social Partners on *parental leave* and *part-time work*.

The concept of minimum social standards in the European Union domestic market bears witness to an undeniable fact: The economic performance capacity and the social welfare state constitutions of the member states are very different. The large majority of the European Union social policy guidelines are, therefore, dominated mostly by the principle of the lowest common denominator. In comparison to the labour and social policy standards of the more developed social states (e.g. Sweden, Denmark, Germany), the European norms are often weaker. Exceptions are constituted perhaps by the prevention principle enshrined in the European Union law on the Work Environment, the computer screen work guideline, and the policies on equality of treatment of women.

Treaty of Amsterdam:
European employment strategy and integration of the social protocol

In 1997, the government of Tony Blair ended the British opt-out in the area of social policy. The Amsterdam Treaty contained a separate Title VIII '*Employment*'. Thus it became possible to coordinate the national employment policies of the member states on the basis of European guidelines. The member states were obliged to prepare yearly *National Action Plans* for implementing these guidelines. However, the guidelines primarily contained non-binding recommendations.

At the same time, with a new Title XI '*Social policy, general and professional education and youth*', the European Union social policy areas previously contained in the Social Agreement and the Social Protocol were integrated into the treaty, reordered anew and partly extended. Included were topics such as health and safety at the workplace, working conditions, professional qualifications; equality of opportunity between men and women in the labour market, equal treatment at the workplace and equality of wages without sex discrimination; social security and social protection of working people, information and consultation for employees, collective bargaining, promotion of employment and much more. The new Article 13 of the Amsterdam Treaty for the first time enabled legislative and other initiatives of the European Union to fight 'discrimination based on sex, race, ethnic origin, religion or belief, disability, age or sexual orientation.'

As a result of the Amsterdam Treaty the following social policy fields of action now became subject to a majority decision in the Council:

- employment policy guidelines,
- improvement of the working environment (employment protection and security at the workplace),
- working conditions,
- information and consultation for employees,
- equality of opportunity of men and women in the labour market, equal treatment at the workplace and equal compensation for equal and equivalent labour,
- provisions for the realisation of the European Social Funds.

For all others, there continued to operate the unanimity rule. Questions of wages, and industrial action continued to be excluded. In the area of struggle against social marginalisation, the Council was given the right to take initiatives for cooperation between the member states with respect to improving the state of knowledge, the exchange of information, and proven procedures for the promotion of innovative approaches and of the evaluation of the experiences encountered.

The Lisbon Summit and the Treaty of Nice: Method of open coordination

This procedure was called into being by the European Union summit in Lisbon in 2000, under the title *'method of open coordination'* as a more general instrument of governmental cooperation in various areas of policy. It departs from the assumption that for the policy area concerned (as here, for example, the fight against social exclusion), the level of the national state retains the prime responsibility. The coordination at the European Union level implies first of all the systematic gathering of information and drawing up comparisons of 'proven practices' of member states. On this basis, it became possible to lay down meaningful indicators permitting a more systematic comparison between the member states (the so-called 'benchmarking').

In a further step, general principles and goals or more concrete European guidelines for European coordination (as has already been done with the European employment policy) can be adopted by the Council . This may lead to member states committing themselves to national action plans. In these, they describe how their measures taken at the national level will serve the implementation of the goals and principles agreed at the European level. In the area of the fight against social exclusion, the Council has decided, for example, in favour of very generally formulated European goals and principles, with the member states committing themselves to national action plans of a two-year duration. On the basis of experiences with the national action plans, there then takes place a common and reciprocal evaluation. The method of open coordination is therefore a legally non-binding European procedure ('soft law approach'). It leads to no sanctions in the case that the implementation of the European goals does not succeed, or worked only inadequately. It is therefore an indirect European steering method which basically relies on the common elaboration of a European guiding model and European goals (substantiated by 'indicators'). The member states are subject to pressure inasmuch as the governments have to make explanations to one another, to the Commission and to the media, as to whether their policies correspond to the European guiding models. Put briefly, 'black sheep' can be identified and pilloried.

The Treaty of Nice (2001) again modified the provisions concerning European social policy. It listed the following fields of action (*italic*: unanimity principle in the Council):

a) improvement, especially of the working environment for the protection of health and the safety of those employed,
b) working conditions,
c) *social security and social protection of those employed,*
d) *protection of workers and employees in case of termination of work contract,*
e) information and consultation with those employed,
f) *representation and collective perception of the interests of the working people and of the employers, including co-determination rights, subject to paragraph 5,*
g) *employment conditions of the citizens of third countries, who are legal residents on the territory of the community,*
h) occupational integration of the persons excluded from the labour market, irrespective of Article 150 (supplemental European measures for professional education),
i) equality of opportunities between men and women in the labour market and equal treatment at work,
j) fight against social exclusion,
k) Modernisation of the systems of social protection, irrespective of c) above.

In all of these fields of action, the Council may decide on initiatives in accordance with the open method of coordination, whereby a European harmonisation of legal prescriptions is explicitly excluded. In the areas a) to i), the Council may in addition enact European guidelines with minimal stipulations. These minimal standards, however, should prescribe 'no administrative, financial or legal burdens hindering the start-up and development of small and medium-sized businesses.' As a rule, it decides by qualified majority, except in the areas c), d), f) and g).

The European Union summit in Nice had also passed the Charter of Basic Rights – however, only as a legally non-binding 'solemn declaration'. The Basic Charter also contains economic and social basic rights, which will bind the institutions of the European Union and its policies in all areas, and it is planned that it will be possible to sue for them on an individual basis before the European Court of Justice. The content of social and economic basic rights in this context is comparatively moderate, in many respects even disappointing. The *European Social Charter of the European Council* with its 31 articles contains a much more precise description of basic social rights. It more strongly emphasises the equal treatment of women in all areas, the compatibility of profession and private life, the right to dignified working conditions and preventive protection of the working environment and health, the right to protection against poverty and social exclusion, and the right to a home.

The Draft Constitution by the European Convention (2003)

With the draft of a 'Constitution for Europe' (July 2003), the European Convention tried to anchor the Charter of Basic Rights in a legally binding manner as the second part of the constitution. This endeavour was supported by all European governments. Apart from that, the draft of the constitution carried out changes relevant to European social policy essentially in the area of goals of the European Union (Part 1 of the Draft).

In Article 3, Paragraph 3 of Part 1 of the Constitutional Draft, it was made clear that 'The Union shall work for the sustainable development of Europe based on balanced economic growth, a social market economy, highly competitive and aiming at full employment and social progress, and with a high level of protection and improvement of the quality of the environment. It shall promote scientific and technical advance.

It shall combat social exclusion and discrimination and shall promote social justice and protection, equality between women and men, solidarity between generations, and protection of children's rights.

It shall promote economic, social, and territorial cohesion and solidarity among member states.'

While, for example, the goals of a 'social market economy' and of 'full employment and social progress' are new, it is noticeable that there is no longer, as in the now operative Treaty of Nice, the question of a '*high degree* of social protection' (Article 2, ECT).

In Article 14, it is determined moreover that the Union may 'adopt initiatives to ensure coordination of Member States' social policies'.

In Part III of the Constitutional Draft (Policy Areas), there then no longer is the question of social market economy, full employment and so on. It contains, in essence, the already valid stipulations and formulations of the Nice Treaty. Thus it appears that the European Union Constitution has brought no substantial innovation in the area of social policy. On the contrary: the neoliberal economic policy of the 'open market' and the priority of free competition are elevated into constitutional rank and also threaten to erode the already existing social and employment policy orientations, and to make their realisation impossible.

Interim balance

As a preliminary balance of the *'integration method of the competitive state'* since the mid-1980s (creation of the domestic market, preparation and implementation of the economic and currency union and the Euro, deepening of the domestic market by way of 'structural reforms' of the goods, services, capital and labour markets in the direction of liberalisation and flexibilisation, creation of an integrated European financial market by the year 2005), where stands social policy?

- 'Social policy concerns' have been symbolically integrated, especially with the Treaty of Amsterdam (under the headings 'Employment', 'Social Policy', 'General and Professional Education and Youth'), majority decisions have been partially extended, and the 'European coordination' of corresponding policies of the national states has been made possible (employment policy guidelines, treaty stipulations of Nice) ;
- As before, social policy in its core remains the competence of the national states; the European coordination processes are largely non-binding;
- The legislative activity of the European Union retains gaps and is constrained to 'minimum prescriptions', which quite often remain well below the practices of the member states with more developed social policies.

European social policy thus disposes neither of considerable financial resources, nor does it take on any redistributive function. The social and employment policy coordination processes also do not even require member states to invest more resources in these areas at the national level. The European Union limited itself at first to a social regulatory policy (social minimum standards in the domestic market). Their vigour, however, has already lost a lot of steam since the end of the 1990s (hardly any new European guideline projects concerning 'minimum prescriptions'). Instead, a 'coordination' has developed, which is designed to steer social policy indirectly.

II
The 'European Social Model' – myth or reality?

In the documents of the institutions of the European Union (Commission, Council, European Parliament) there is always the question of a 'European social model', which would be clearly distinguishable from the social models of the United States and Japan. The European Commission defined the European social model as follows: 'it is characterised by democracy and rights of the individual, absence of tariffs, market economy, equal chances for each and everyone as well as social security and solidarity' (White Book Social Policy 1994). The European Trade Union Confederation provided an even more resolute definition: 'This model, which is characterised by a very high level of social protection grounded in solidarity, by the central role of public services, the high status of collective agreements and various models of co-determination, is based on the indispensable compromise between market forces and the democratic state' (ETUC 1995).

As a matter of fact, expenditure on social protection in the EU-15 was at about 27.3% of the European Union Gross Domestic Product in 2000, and thus higher than in the United States with its 14-17% of GDP, or in Japan, which spends 12-15% of its GDP (1991-98). This is also due to structural differences in the respective constitutions of the social state. In Japan, for example, social security is organised much more (but at a decreasing level) by way of the life-long work-place guarantee for core employees and corresponding contributions by the firm, and much less by way of public social security systems. In the United States, while there exists, as a result of the New Deal by Franklin D. Roosevelt in the 1930s and the *War on Poverty* Programme by Lyndon B. Johnson in the 1960s, a rudimentary social state (minimal state pension insurance and unemployment benefits, various credit facilities in favour of low-income households for education, housing or acquisition of residential property as well as for small farmers, and so on), there is, for instance, no social health insurance covering the whole population.

The social state and the level of social protection in Western Europe are, in fact, as a result of the greater strength of the organised labour movement and its struggles in the 19th and 20th centuries as well as systemic competition, more strongly developed and as a rule better equipped with resources than in the United States or Japan. On the road to capitalist modernity, the battle lines between the social classes in Europe assumed a clearer shape than elsewhere. A party system, historically built upon the class antagonisms (with smaller and larger parties in the traditions of the labour movement and the bourgeoisie), and a relatively pronounced class-determined electoral and strike pattern are still typical in Western Europe. In the United States, there exists up to now no mass party which would base itself upon the traditions of the labour movement, and in Japan, these parties are, as a rule, too weak to exercise any influence on the formation of the government and the design of state policy.

Beyond these statements, however, there exists very little support for the thesis of a more or less *unified* 'European social model'. 'Democracy, personal rights, and the market economy' can also be claimed by the capitalistically constituted societies of the United States and Japan. In the USA as well, structures of publicly regulated service (*Public Utility Regulation*) and programmes for equality of opportunity (*Affirmative Action*), as the inheritance of the New Deal and the War on Poverty, played a certain role. Their status and the scope of their applicability, however, are very different even within Europe. The latter holds to an even greater extent for co-determination and comprehensive collective agreements.

Diversity of welfare state models in the European Union

On the basis of empirical examinations at the beginning of the 1990s (Esping-Andersen 1990), one can establish that about four different welfare state models exist side by side:

- The *Mediterranean or rudimentary welfare state* (e.g. Greece, Portugal,

Spain): it includes a tax-financed, general state health system, but weak social insurance systems with little flexibility. The traditional family structures still play an important role as social support system; countrywide minimal protection systems, on the other hand, barely exist.

- The *liberal welfare state* (e.g. Great Britain, Ireland and – yes – the United States): it is based upon a universal, mostly tax-financed social security, which is designed only to avoid extreme poverty, and a strict system of means testing, leading to a 'hole-riddled' support with low transfer intensity. All tasks of social security going beyond poverty prevention are organised, if at all, by business or state sponsoring or private supplementary insurance policies.
- The *conservative-corporatist welfare state* (e.g. France, Federal Republic of Germany, Austria, Italy since the 1980s): It is tied predominantly to gainful employment and relies on contribution-financed, income-dependent social security systems with moderate redistributive mechanisms which are supposed to maintain the customary social status and standard of living. It relies on the ideal of the life-long, full-time employed male family head of household (with correspondingly weak and inadequate social protection for 'atypical' earners) and offers a tax-financed minimal social protection with a means test for those who cannot be integrated into the labour market and have no other sources of income.
- The *social-democratic welfare state* (e.g. Sweden, Denmark). It relies on a universal, predominantly tax-financed social security system with transfer intensity and comparatively high redistribution. The systems are aimed at a policy of equality, which also includes the equal positioning of the sexes, coupled with the large extension of social infrastructural institutions (infant care, all-day schools, and so on). Added to that are supplementary, contribution-financed insurance systems, especially company-level pension systems regulated legally or by collective agreement.

The West European welfare states are for the most part distinguished according to two ideal-typical principles: the *Bismarck principle* (which rests classically upon *contribution-financed social insurances* and is thus centred upon gainful employment) and the *Beveridge principle* (which classically relies on *tax-financed, universal minimal protection*). Each of the national welfare states in the European Union, however, represent specific mixtures of the Bismarck and the Beveridge types. Even in the classical country of the Bismarck-type, the Federal Republic of Germany, social security is financed from general tax revenue. In classical countries of the Beveridge type (such as Great Britain and Denmark), unemployment support is based on contribution-financed social insurance. In this respect, the historically grown welfare-state regulations in the West European countries of the European Union are distinguished by great diversity and show clear differences in the scope of the services, the structure and the financing rules of the social systems.

Table 1: Financing Social Security
(according to types of revenues, in % of the total financed amount)

	Tax-financed *(public budgets)*		Social insurance contributions						Others	
			Total		*Employers*		*Insured*			
	1991	**2000**	**1991**	**2000**	**1991**	**2000**	**1991**	**2000**	**1991**	**2000**
EU-15	**30.9**	**35.8**	**65.0**	**60.7**	**41.4**	**38.3**	**23.6**	**22.4**	**4.1**	**3.5**
B	21.4	25.3	69.4	72.3	43.7	49.5	25.7	22.8	9.2	2.5
DK	81.7	63.9	11.7	29.4	7.2	9.1	4.5	20.3	6.6	6.7
D	26.9	32.5	70.5	65.2	42.2	36.9	28.3	28.2	2.6	2.4
EL	32.8	29.1	58.4	60.8	38.1	38.2	20.3	22.6	8.8	10.1
E	27.3	26.9	69.9	69.1	53.2	52.7	16.7	16.4	2.7	4.0
F	17.6	30.6	78.8	66.5	50.4	45.9	28.3	20.6	3.6	2.9
IRL	60.0	58.3	38.9	40.2	24.0	25.0	15.0	15.1	1.0	1.5
I	29.1	39.8	68.7	58.1	52.6	43.2	16.1	14.9	2.2	2.1
L	40.6	47.1	51.9	48.4	29.8	24.6	22.1	23.8	7.5	4.5
NL	23.9	14.2	60.4	67.9	20.1	29.1	40.3	38.8	15.7	17.9
A	35.7	35.3	63.2	63.8	38.1	37.1	25.1	26.8	1.2	0.3
P	26.1	38.7	60.9	53.5	41.8	35.9	19.1	17.6	13.0	7.3
FIN	44.1	43.1	48.1	49.8	40.9	37.7	7.2	12.1	7.8	7.1
S	n.a.	46.7	n.a.	49.1	n.a.	39.7	n.a.	9.4	n.a.	4.3
UK	44.6	47.1	53.7	51.6	27.9	30.2	25.8	21.4	1.7	1.3

Source; Eurostat-ESSPROS 2003;
B = Belgium, **DK** = Denmark, **D**= Germany, **EL**= Greece, **E**= Spain; **F**= France, **IRL**= Ireland, **I** = Italy, **L**= Luxemburg, **NL** = Netherlands, **A**= Austria, **P**= Portugal, **FIN**= Finland, **S**= Sweden, **UK**= Great Britain

In May 2004, the European Union was extended by the addition of ten new member states, predominantly from Eastern Europe. The new East European member states, until 1989/91, had belonged to the 'real socialist' camp and had had a social security system corresponding to this type of society. In the 1990s, they experienced a far-reaching transformation of their economic and social system, in the course of which different variants of a market-radical 'shock therapy' were being tried on them. In contrast to the highfalutin promises of fast and durable welfare for everybody, the transformation to a market economy in all Eastern European countries at first led to a drastic slump in the gross domestic product. Only in the year 2000, four of these countries – Poland, Hungary, Slovenia and Slovakia – were able to significantly surpass the level of their 'real-socialist' gross domestic product of 1989. The Czech Republic (98%) and the Baltic states of Estonia, Latvia and Lithuania were still below it. The European backlog of the Central and East European states in comparison to the European Union measured by their gross domestic product, or rather industrial and agricultural production, was larger in the year 2000 than it had been in 1989. Half the new member states reach a gross domestic product per capita of over 50% of the EU-15 average (of those, only Slovenia and Cyprus achieve 70% or more). The other half lies clearly below the European Union average. In comparison to the earlier Southern extension (Spain, Portugal and Greece), the new enlargement of the European Union brings significantly more dramatic gaps in welfare and in the level of economic development.

European Union enlargement 2004:
the Falling EU social security quota

The social security systems of the new member states are organised on similar structural principles to those in the 'old' EU states, but typically at a very low level of protection. Most of them arrange social protection according to the insurance principle (Bismarck type), while social security-type payments are financed by general taxes and are contingent on a means test. Estonia finances the public pension and health system by a social tax (Beveridge type), while unemployment benefits are organised like an insurance. Next to these more general structural features, there remains, however, as in the old European Union, a great variety in the scope of payments, the concrete financing structure, and the distribution of burdens between employees and employers concerning social security contributions. A number of states (Slovenia, Hungary, Czech Republic, Estonia) rely on enrolment in company-level pension schemes (voluntary or obligatory). In health care as well, there exist different regulations concerning entitlements, additional insurances, and private supplemental payments.[2]

For a number of middle and East European new member states, it is clear, however, that the provision of social security services is 'full of holes' and precarious, and that in particular the problems of growing poverty and social exclusion receive little attention. In Poland, for instance, the real unemployment rate has risen to 20%, but only a fifth of the unemployed receive unemployment benefit.

Table 2:
Public Social Expenditures as a Percentage of the GDP (Social Performance Quota) in the EU

Country	1991	1993	2000
EU-Average	**26.4**	**28.8**	**27.3**
Austria	27.0	28.9	28.7
Belgium	27.1	29.3	26.7
Denmark	29.7	31.9	28.8
Germany	26.1	28.4	29.5
Greece	21.6	22.1	26.4
Finland	29.8	34.6	25.2
France	28.4	30.7	29.7
Ireland	19.6	20.2	14.1
Italy	25.2	26.4	25.2
Luxemburg	22.5	23.7	21.0
Netherlands	32.6	33.6	27.4
Portugal	17.2	21.0	22.7
Spain	21.2	24.0	20.1
Sweden	34.3	39.0	32.3
United Kingdom	25.7	29.0	26.8

Source: Eurostat-ESSPROS 2003.

Already for the first 15 EU member states, the level of public social expenditures in comparison to their respective gross domestic product (the social performance quota) is very different: it ranges from 14.1% in Ireland to 32.3% in Sweden. The Mediterranean states (Portugal, Spain,

Table 3:
Public Social Expenditures as a Percentage of GDP (Social Performance Quota) in the New Member States (plus States joining later)

Important note: This table contains ***preliminary data****; due to a lack of 'harmonisation' of different national definitions of social protection expenditures, there still are no absolutely comparable data;*

Country	**1998**	**2000**
Estonia	14.7	15.2
Latvia	17.6	17.8
Lithuania	15.8	15.8
Poland	23.9	24.0
Hungary	24.2	23.2
Slovakia	21.9	21.7
Slovenia	26.1	n.a.
Czechia	18.1	19.5
Cyprus	12.8	n.a.
Malta	19.6	19.8
EU-10 (new member states)*		**19.6**
1.1 EU-25		**23.2**
Bulgaria (2007)	14.9	17.9
Romania (2007)	13.8	13.9
Turkey	10.4	10.6
1.2 EU-28		**22.3**

Source: GVG Study on the Social Protection Systems in the 13 Applicant Countries, Synthesis Report, Second Draft, November 2002

* Where data for 2000 were lacking (Slovenia, Cyprus), the 1998 data were used for the calculation of the respective averages (EU-10, EU-25, EU-28)

Greece) have caught up to a significant extent since the 1980s, but there still persists a noticeable gap with the richer European Union states.

The social performance quotas of most of the new member states lie clearly below this level – the average for the ten new member states for the year 2000 yields a social performance quota of 19.6%. In contrast to the Southern extension of the European Union, the present enlargement is taking place without expansion of the structural funds. On the contrary, the new member states in the beginning will receive only 25% of the agricultural subsidies due to them; only over the next ten years will the figure grow gradually to 100%. In the political debate about the European Union budget and the financial framework 2006-2011, Germany in particular is pushing for a further lowering of the budgetary limit (to 1% or at a maximum 1.1% of the EU GDP) or at least for a freeze at the present level. If this line prevails, the new member states will be left on their own with the task of coping with structural changes in industry and the catching up to European Union levels of welfare.

In the middle – and amongst East European new member countries, around 20% of employment is in agriculture – in the EU-15, it is on average only 4.3%. Added to that will be the foreseeable structural change in the old industrial regions (mining, steel and shipyards, and so on) and with unemployment rates already at double the average. With this background, we can expect a clear increase in unemployment and socio-political problems in the new member states, for the solution of which no resources are planned. Whether a catching-up of social performance levels will be possible under these conditions appears extremely questionable. It is much more likely that the average social performance level of the extended European Union will drift clearly in the direction of that of the United States. The idea of a superior 'European social model' is still defensible on the grounds that the European Union guarantees a significantly higher social protection level than the United States, but under these pressures this thesis will become much more shaky.

III
Modernisation of the Welfare State: The re-evaluation of 'social justice'

The development of the social state is often interpreted as a large-scale social experiment designed to solve the social or workers' question. Up until the late modern period, social policy was concentrated predominantly upon caring for the poor. This was usually done by charitable organisations of the various Christian churches or religious communities or of the educated middle classes and was suffused with assumptions concerning the proper conduct of the poor. An example is the institution of the late modern age 'workhouse' (18th and early 19th century), in which poor people were interned, instructed in 'useful' industrial cultural techniques, and driven to forced labour.[3]

From the care for the poor to the rudimentary social state

The process of urbanisation accelerated by manufacture and industrial revolution led to the development of state hygiene policies. Their goal was to secure public health and to fight against epidemics. This was after all in the state interest, since it would improve defence and financial capacity. The development of statistics (especially health, social and age statistics) created a decisive technical prerequisite for organisation and work on the problems of developing industrial society from the early part of the 19th century. Social statistics and the probability calculus laid the foundation for the realisation amongst bureaucratic-scientific circles that the social risks (illness, unemployment, accidents, invalidity, the illnesses of old-age, and so on) of capitalist industrial society could not be explained by mere accidents, the blind rage of evil powers or the individual guilt of some, but resulted from the objective facts of social communal life. A state regulated insurance for compensating these social risks (as a 'social insurance' or financed from tax revenue) seemed ever more necessary, coupled with a policy of prevention (security and health protection at the work-place, and so on). On the side of the labour movement, the experiences of self-help insurances and support associations (collective security against loss of wages due to the failure of working capacity or closure of the workplace) played a role, which, due to the rather limited number of members and the voluntary basis of these associations, had remained precarious.

This new perception of social risks could only impose itself very gradually. A very important role in this respect was played by the growth of the organised labour movement, which the establishment perceived as a potential threat. The growing (socialist, anarcho-syndicalist and anarchist) workers' movement in Europe demanded the material realisation of the principles of the bourgeois revolution – *liberté, égalité, fraternité.* It insisted on an extension of democratic participation rights (women and general electoral law), on a turning away from the demeaning 'care' for the poor, and above all on a radical change of primary distribution and the overcoming of the capitalist private ownership of the means of production. The official majority position of the social-democratic/socialist parties held a social revolution to be inevitable. It would follow from the 'collapse of capitalism', which was bound to happen according to quasi natural-law-like rules. This attitude has rightfully been called 'revolutionary party on hold' or 'revolutionary waiting stance'. At the same time, there also existed in the labour movement an alternative strategy of 'gradual reforms', which received great support especially in the leading apparatuses of the more moderate trade unions. These reforms were supposed to be introduced by governmental coalitions with social-liberal or radical democratic bourgeois forces, as for example in France after the Dreyfus affair, in 1899, by the government coalition for the 'Defence of the Republic'.

The breakthrough to state social security legislation and the introduction of rudimentary social insurance in Germany under Bismarck took place from 1878 to 1890, with the aim of halting the rise of the labour movement and social democracy. As an accompanying measure to the health and accident insurance legislation, and the introduction of a pension and invalidity insurance as obligatory for workers and 'small' employees, social democracy was banned and subjected to measures of repression. Old-age pensions were granted after 30 years of contribution and were designed as a partial pension, which was supposed to allow a certain reduction in work activity. However, not even one-third of all men reached 70 years of age.

Although the social insurance principle is attributed to him, Bismarck personally had at least in the matter of old age insurance championed a tax-financed minimal insurance system with the primary goal of poverty prevention. Bismarck repeatedly compared the 'soldier of work' with the soldier in the army – both should be tied to the state by way of a (minimal) state pension. The authoritarian-paternalistic bent of bourgeois social reform is unmistakable. Austrian and British governments from 1906 to 1914 followed with similar minimalist social reforms (old age security, employment exchanges, accident and health insurance).

The further rise of the trade union and labour workers' movement could not stop the Bismarckian double strategy of political repression and gradual social reform. As a result, after a hesitant start, the bourgeois social reform in Europe, however, evoked different political responses in the workers' movement. 'Revisionist' and reformist currents in trade unions and parties seized on the offer to at least influence the 'secondary distribution' through an extension of the social sphere, and new social rights in the framework of a rationally-guided 'modernisation' of the bourgeois state and the expansion of large industrial concerns and monopolies by way of a step-by-step strategy for social progress (work and social legislation, extension of social insurances and the claims linked to them, works' council and 'industrial democracy', standardisation of gainful employment, and so on). The 'old' conflict over the socialisation of the means of production and a new mode of production was deferred.

Quite essential for the growth of these reformist streams was the incapacity of the traditional strategy of 'revolutionary waiting stance' to stop the outbreak of war fever, fuelled by nationalism, which infected working people as well as others at the outbreak of World War One, or to use the collapse after the end of the war for a revolutionary transformation in Europe towards the old goals of the workers' movement. The 'reformist' majority social democracy acted rather as a stabilising force in the restoration of capitalism in Europe after the war. In that endeavour, it was quite able in the beginning to achieve partial successes in at least some countries (the 8-hour-day, works' councils, housing policy in Austria, and so on) and to extend the social state. The 'Communist' fraction of the workers' movement remained a minority in Western Europe. In the late 1920s and in the 1930s, the social state achievements came under pressure. From the increasing social polarisation, fascism in some countries of Western Europe was strengthened, then buried parliamentary democracy and initiated a new World War.

The 'Keynesian Welfare State' after the Second World War

The breakthrough to the social state 'as we know it' came only after the end of the Second World War. The ideological and conceptual blueprint for that was not delivered by the socialist-social democratic labour movement (except in the Swedish case), but by social liberalism (Keynes, Beveridge). Keynes turned against monetarism and the *laissez-faire* politics prevailing in the inter-war period, which had led to deflation, mass unemployment, polarisation of incomes and a *rentier* economy. Instead, a state interventionist macroeconomic policy was necessary, which would strengthen mass purchasing power and final demand, thereby stimulating productive investment and moving the economy in the direction of a full employment equilibrium. The state should not become the owner of the means of production, but should, via macroeconomic policy and investment guidance in periods of economic stagnation, counteract the underemployment of capacities and resources. In this way both the capitalist ownership structure and parliamentary democracy could be saved – against fascism from the right and Bolshevism from the left.

From the point of view of learning theory, Keynes' strategy amounts to the creation of 'win-win'-constellations: state interventionism ought to secure a reliable environment for profitable enterprises, higher wages for workers and full employment. As a result of this 'class compromise', it would be possible to secure the viability of the capitalist economy, while at the same time maintaining relative social peace, reduced inequality of income and improved social security for the employed. This basic philosophy also came into play through the Beveridge plan for the great social state reform in Britain. It was picked up by the bourgeois parties as well as by the reformist parties of the labour movement, even if with different emphases. In fact, in Western Europe, after the Second World War, it was predominantly bourgeois majority parties which promoted the extension of the social state.

The 'Keynesian welfare state' was no longer limited to protective measures against the classical social risks of a capitalist earnings-based society (accident, invalidity, health, old age, unemployment, poverty, protection of motherhood, and so on), but took on extended tasks for the stabilisation of the overall economy (macroeconomic politics) and the achievement of 'social cohesion' (educational expansion, policies of equal opportunities, employment and social policies, construction of affordable housing, regional policy for levelling up living conditions, promotion of culture, and so on).

The welfare state and different ideas of 'justice'

The concrete design of the welfare states after the Second World War followed specific national patterns, which contained country-specific mixtures of in each case partly diverging, partly supplemental guiding principles of social justice (compare also Esping-Andersen's typology). From the tradition of care for the poor comes the principle of *need orientation*: social payments tested case by case according to the income and family situation of the person concerned. On the bourgeois postulate of formal equality and the idea of the commonweal, comes the principle of *justice according to need* : securing of socially acceptable minimum support, which is supposed to insure the maximum possible participation of all in social life (approach of provisioning). The liberal postulate of individual liberty and the welfare of the individual is based on the principle of *justice according to performance*.

Social policy aligned with egalitarianism, moreover, aims at the reduction of wealth and income differentials ('material equality politics', mainly through progressive taxation of income and wealth), as well as *equality of opportunity* and anti-discrimination measures (education, women, immigrants, disabled people, and so on). The American philosopher John Rawls has introduced the *difference principle* into the debate on equality: social and economic inequality is tolerable as long as distribution is shaped in such a way that the poorest classes also take part in economic growth (the elevator principle). The difference principle is thus a typical image of the Fordist 'welfare-through-growth philosophy'. The *justice for stability* incorporates a rather more pragmatic principle: securing relative 'social peace', prevention of revolts, and so on.

Bismarck's social state policy was motivated to a large extent by the notion of justice for stability – the workers were to be held back from their aspirations of fundamental revolutionary change. The social state concept of Beveridge was inspired predominantly by the idea of justice according to need: guarantee of a national income minimum as a benchmark of social state activity. The principle of justice according to performance held for him at the enterprise level, with private prevention to be built on that. Adenauer, on the other hand, anchored the principle of justice according to performance in the concept of dynamic pension insurance. It relied on the right of all employed people to adequate security of their standard of living through the state system in old age.

Already the most basic forms of social state regulation – insurance protection against social risks – made it necessary to formulate general principles, which would distinguish between risks for which the individual had to cover, and those which were to be compensated by social insurance companies or other state instruments. Compensation for the risks covered by social insurance was thereby formulated as individual legal rights. They had to rank as inalienable, and it must be possible for those entitled to claim them legally from the state or the social insurance authorities. In parallel, there developed conceptions of economic, social, and cultural rights, which would be guaranteed by the democratic social state in accordance with the applicable specific social norms and be attributed by its various instruments individually and collectively (as claims to compensation, income, provision of public and social services, and so on).

The Scandinavian, social-democratic welfare state tradition is especially inspired by the concept of indisputable legal claims, which are tied in a universalist fashion to state citizenship. In other traditions, this principle of universal social citizenship rights is far more fractured. Means-test-based services (such as social and unemployment compensation) only represent the right to *access* a service. The principle of *subsidiarity* (taking into account the income of other persons when calculating services, and so on) further constrains this right of access. In particular, social insurance systems centred on gainful employment often set the 'male family head of household' as a norm, from which there result only *derived claims* (for example, to widow and orphan protection, and so on).

Controversial interpretations of the contradictions of the Keynesian welfare state

The Keynesian welfare state in its different national incarnations has often remained divided in Western Europe. Social services and social insurance, the social cushion against poverty, fiscal and workplace-related payments have all developed in an unequal fashion. They brought an after-the-fact correction to market results and social welfare, but they also produced under-supply and exclusion ('marginalised fringe groups', 'new poverty').

Given this background, it is no surprise that the social and welfare state became subject to different interpretations and modifications:

- *Class-theory*, there was – with respect to the welfare state – the question 'of an asymmetrical class compromise and a partial integration of the workers' movement into the capitalist society. *Asymmetrical*, since the representation of dominant interests in capitalist societies is structurally superior to the representation of working class interests; *partial integration*, since the workers' movement even under an emphatically non-revolutionary oriented leadership continues to strive beyond capitalist society' (von Oertzen 1984).
- *modernisation-theory* – in 'right' as well as 'left' variants – the increase in social complexity, the extension of state oversight, risk insurance and prevention, and growing legalisation, increase in the application of scientific methods and professionalism, all come to the fore. This scenario presupposes the development of a differentiation and segmentation of the 'clients' of the social state. Negative aspects of the social state would be the bureaucratic 'intervention' in life spheres (child rearing, care for the elderly, and so on), a colonisation of life-styles by the value system on which social services are based and the definition of needs by professionals. On that basis, contradictions and conflicts can be expected to develop: the social state could quite possibly intensify the problems which it is supposed to cure.
- *From the point of view of democracy theory*, the social and welfare state is interpreted as social innovation, by which the definition of

> unconditional legal claims and universal social claims, as well as instruments for their material realisation, makes possible the participation on an equal basis of all citizens in the processes of political, democratic self-determination in the first place. In this view, social protection only creates the material basis for the political autonomy of state citizens, independent of their role in the democratic process.

From the presentation up until now, it also follows, that the Keynesian welfare state had understood serious economic and social crises as 'exceptional situations'. It was after all geared towards a trajectory with steadily high economic growth, growing labour productivity and high mass consumption, which meant that the social net would only be under strain during temporary declines in economic activity. The defenders of an all too simple interpretation of Keynes' theory were, unsurprisingly, hard hit, when in the mid-1970s, with almost complete full employment, a rapid inflation of goods prices and wages (wage-price-spiral) went along with an abrupt halt in economic growth (stagflation), and economic growth rates flattening over the next decades.

Graph 1: Economic Growth in the EU-15, 1960-2003

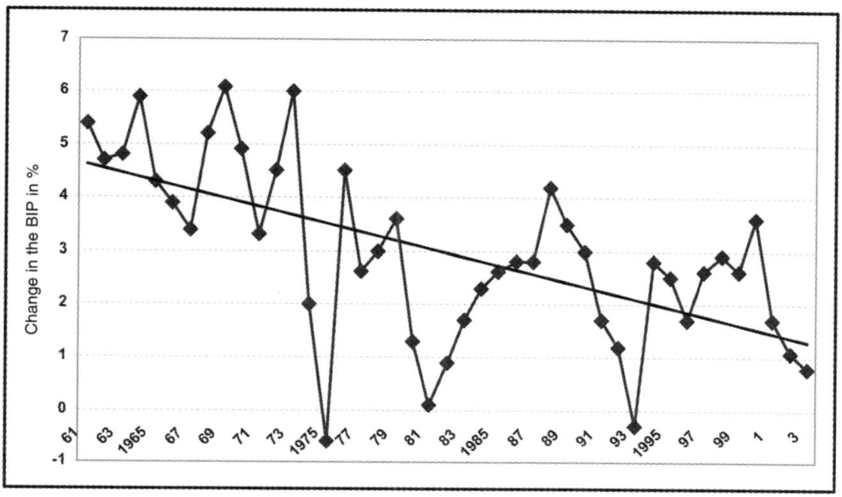

Source: European Economy No. 71, 2001, Statistical Appendix, Table 3, European Economy: Autumn Forecast 2003, Statistical Annex, Table 1.

In his essay on *'The long term problem of unemployment,'* Keynes had dealt in 1943 (thus in the middle of World War Two) with the problem of what to do when investment demand is satisfied to the extent that it can no longer be lifted back to the indicated savings level (thus the one compatible with full employment; *A.B.*), without engaging upon wasteful or unnecessary undertakings. His answer was to promote sensible consumption, disapprove of savings, and compensate for a part of the unwanted excess supply by increased leisure, more holidays and shorter working hours. This answer placed the main emphasis of the solution on the 'question of distribution'. Beyond that, it pointed to larger questions of quality of life and emancipation, which then in the mid-1970s were raised by the feminist movement, the milieu of the '68ers, the revolt of the skilled workers against the stupid Fordist work organisation (*blue collar blues*), and the emerging environmental movement. Keynes' concept would have required a break with the support of the previously valid 'class compromise', whereby essentially only increases in growth count as redistributive

Graph 2:
Wages as a proportion of National Income in the EU 15, 1960 – 2002

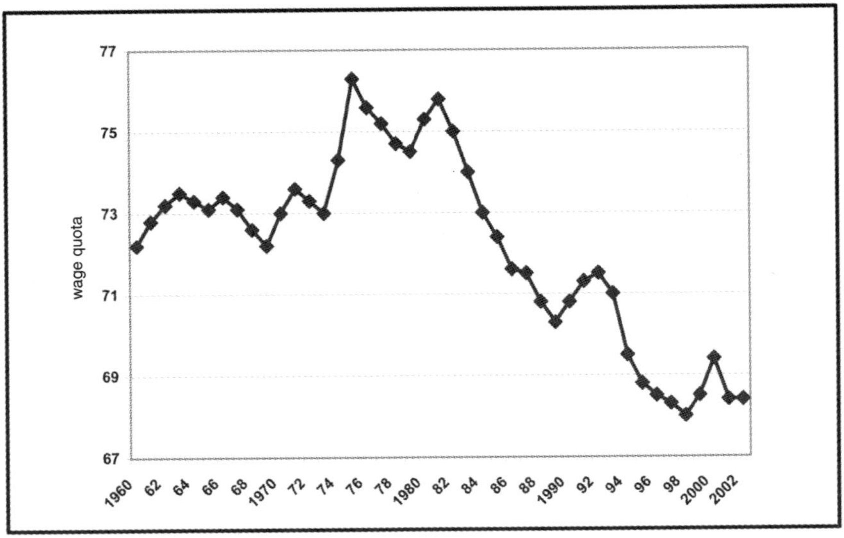

Source: European Economy, No. 73, 2001, p. 358 f.

mass. Before such 'dangerous conclusions' could win a majority, from the point of view of the employers and the wealthy, the emergency brake had to be applied.

In light of this background (and other events in the mid-1970s such as the defeat of the United States in the Vietnam War) it is not surprising that the 'class compromise' now described broke apart and the employers' side switched to the counter offensive with ever more radical and comprehensive social roll back to the restoration of acceptable profit rates, the containment of inflation, the diminishing of 'trade union power' and 'sprawling social state regulation'. As a consequence, there resulted a clear swing in income distribution (reduction in relative wages, with a corresponding increase in profits, in the late 1980s or earlier).

This entrepreneurial offensive found its ideological prop in the economic and social theories of the *neoliberalism of the 1930s and 1940s*, which had remained rather marginal after the Second World War (Hayek, von Mises), and the *monetarism* of the Chicago Boys (Milton

Graph 3: The economy-wide profit rate* in the EU 15, 1960-2002

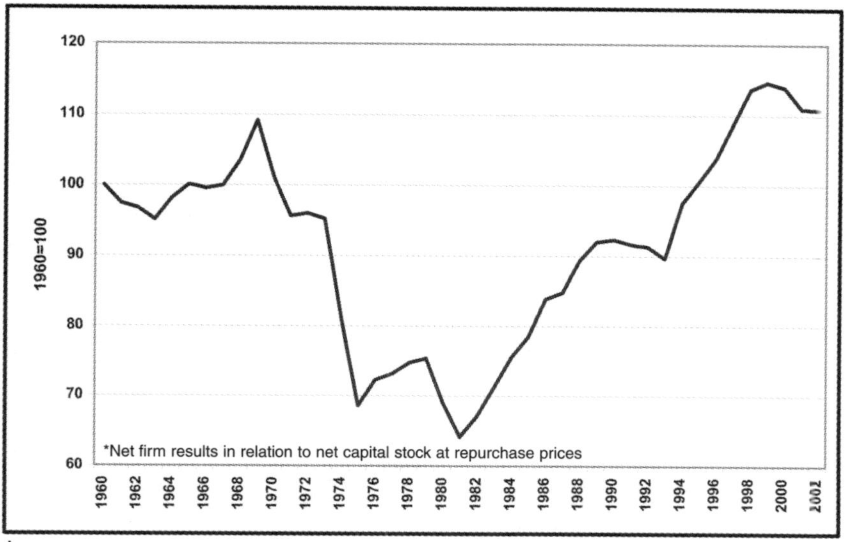

Source: Economy Economy, No. 63, 1997, p. 28, European Commission: EC Economic Data Book, several years, own calculations, Jörg Huffschmid.

Friedman and others). The monetarist economic policy placed above all the fight against inflation and the free operation of market forces at the heart of their strategy – both would by themselves lead to new economic growth and a dynamic economy. The Keynesian full employment policy was laid *ad acta*. The governments of Margaret Thatcher in Britain, Ronald Reagan in the United States and the dictator Augusto Pinochet in Chile were the leading international trailblazers of monetarism.[4]

Controversies around the 'crisis of the welfare state'

In the wake of monetarism and the 'neoliberal revolution', there developed in the 1980s and 1990s various new perspectives on the social state. Some of these are presented in what follows in an 'ideal-typical, stylised' manner:

- The '*pure neoliberal doctrine*' discovered Hayek's old formula of the 'Road to Serfdom' (1944). In its further development, Soviet state socialism, the social democratic welfare state as well as the social state compromises of conservative governments of the post-war period (for example, from Winston Churchill to Edward Heath in Britain; Konrad Adenauer's and Ludwig Ehrhard's 'social market economy' in West Germany; the 'economic programming' of the Gaullists in France) are brandished as variants of 'socialism' stifling the free unfolding of the individual and healthy entrepreneurial spirit, and a new unleashing of market forces is urged. Margaret Thatcher's slogan that 'there is no society, only individuals' epitomises this way of thinking. In the 1990s, this ideology was exemplified by the Future Commission of the Free States of Bavaria and Saxony in the ideological persona of the employee as 'entrepreneur of his/her own labour power'. If only there prevailed sufficient 'economic freedom' and independent responsibility of the individual, the economy could be dynamised in such a way that no more than a basic social security system for women and men incapable of working (citizen money, and so on) would be required.
- On the Marxist-oriented political left, the '*social state illusion*' was attacked. Since the social state did not intervene in the primary distribution and the capitalist property relations, it could not fight the causes of social inequality. Under conditions of flattening

economic growth, it would become increasingly incapable of functioning and would therefore be put into question. Therefore, a change of system towards socialism was required.

- The left tendencies inspired by the '*new social movements*' of the 1980s (Greens, left-wing social democracy sensitised to environmental and women's rights issues, and church circles) raised less these fundamental questions of the alternative social order, than the 'patronising character of the bureaucratic welfare state', its concentration on those in gainful employment, and the far-reaching exclusion of women, socially marginal groups and the 'atypically employed'. A fundamental *reconstruction* was necessary so that the social state would become capable of a future. The visions for overhaul concentrated on the 'recognition' of the up to then marginal interests, an extension of the self-help potential of civil society, and especially on the question of a 'guaranteed basic income' or a 'social basic security' for all. The classical questions of social insurance (securing of living standards in old age, and so on), by contrast, received less attention. A smaller part of this spectrum (in particular from the 'corporativist-conservative welfare states'), at the end of the 1990s, developed vague ideas of the restructuring of social insurance to 'gainfully employed and citizens' insurance', which would no longer be coupled to gainful employment alone (based on the 'Swiss model' of counting in all kinds of incomes for calculation of the financing of social security systems, tax on value creation etc.)
- The mainstream of social democracy (and of the trade unions) had difficulties in locating itself in this new debate on the social state. The first reaction was pragmatic – as much defence of the traditional structures as possible, as much adaptation to weak economic growth rates and 'shrinking state incomes' as necessary. This by the way also held for the 'official' politics of moderate conservatives – cuts in the social safety net were always justified by arguing that only in this way was it possible to maintain the social state in its core and make it capable of having a future. This was certainly also linked with the search for new forms of financing (e.g. the introduction and extension of a general social insurance tax in France on the initiative of the social democratic (socialist) prime

minister Michel Rocard at the beginning of the 1990s) as well as the covering of new risks (for example, the introduction of a old-age care insurance in Germany by the conservatives under social minister Norbert Blüm, whilst abandoning the principle of financing on equal terms by employers and employees).

- Only with the discussion of and pushing through of the '*Strategy of the Third Way*' as the majority position of European social democracy at the end of the 1990s did it dispose of a clear, independent profile. In contrast to the 'true neoliberal doctrine', the 'Third Way' held on to the position that there was such a thing as society. And, under conditions of economic globalisation, a social safety net had to be maintained to catch the 'losers of modernisation' and to carry them into the new conditions. The new basic philosophy said that the state had to steer, not to row. Globalisation and strengthened market forces were expected to bring about a more dynamic economy. The task of the social state would now be to organise equality of opportunity (meaning 'chances at the start', not at the 'finish', as well as a 'second chance' after an initial failure) and possibilities for participation. The unemployed and others dependent on social transfers should, by a system of rights and duties (promote and challenge!) be put into a position to seize the new opportunities arising in a dynamic economy. The social safety net would thereby become a trampoline capable of catapulting the weak and the 'failures' again into economically active employment. For that, an 'activating social state' was needed, which would no longer grant 'passive payments' and 'unconditional claims', but would stress 'incentives' for integration into market activity and the labour market. Reflecting the ideas of the *Communitarians* in the United States, 'society' was understood as 'community', to which individuals in their individual behaviour were accountable: 'On the other hand, there is even a break here with the neoliberal freedom discourse. The priority of *community* as society in the shape of an ethics of duty even denies the purely liberal dimension of freedom. . . Where Thatcher no longer knew whether there was *something like a society,* the society of the national competitive state – in the identification with community – becomes ideologically totalitarian against individuals' (Rheinländer 1999).

Reconstruction or modernisation of the social state: the new confusion

Almost everyone in political and civil society uses similar sounding terms when they talk about the future of the social state: 'reconstruction' (the catch phrase of the 1980s) or 'renewal and modernisation' (the war cry of the 1990s). Ironically, conservatives, liberals and new social democrats increasingly pose in this context as advocates of a 'radical policy' or rather 'system change', while those to the left of them figure as 'keepers of the status quo'. In the political practice of the last 25 years, however, a paradoxical situation can be observed. On the one hand, the ideal-typical thinking patterns outlined above were in part forcefully shaken into new mixes by the political camps. But behind almost identical terms and concepts were often hidden completely different ideas.

Some examples:

- Conservative forces (in West Germany, for example, the CDU under their general secretary Heiner Geissler at the end of the 1970s) seized on the *statism* and bureaucracy critique of the alternative left with the formula of a '*New Social Question*'. The 'old social question' (i.e. the workers' question) had almost settled itself by way of the Keynesian welfare state and the development in living standards of the post-war period. Instead, however, a broad stratum of poor and excluded people had developed on the 'margins of society' (homelessness due to personal crises, poverty due to abundance of children, social exclusion due to handicap, and so on), which could not be prevented with the existing social state structures. In this way, a front was built against the 'disempowering social state', but nothing was changed by government in the 1980s and 1990s to address these problems. On the contrary, the social security systems were slimmed down further.
- The alternative left as well as neoliberal think tanks propagated '*citizens' money*' and the 'negative income tax' as possible forms of a 'social basic insurance'. Often very different things are intended which show themselves only in the proposed level of this basic insurance and the detailed entitlements. The 'lefties' typically want a 'basic income' without any prerequisites, not tied to work

performance, on which it would be possible to live more or less comfortably. The neoliberals, on the other hand, want a 'basic insurance', usually below the poverty line, which would only be granted to citizens 'unfit for work' (or others, if they performed communal tasks or similar chores).

- Conservatives, alternative left-wingers and new social democrats all demand a strengthening and upgrading of *commitment in civil society* and *self-help*. For quite a few alternative lefties, their promotion is an additional task that goes beyond the functions of a renewed social state. They also have to be equipped with additional resources to be realisable. For new social democrats and conservatives self-help structures and civil societal engagement, on the other hand, should increasingly *replace* functions up until then guaranteed by the social state.
- A similar issue is the praise of the '*Third Sector*' and the '*social economy*', which is heard in left, social democratic and even neo-fascist circles. The Italian *Aleanza Nazionale* gives prominence to these notions in its literature and links them to the demolition of state structures and re-evaluation of family, neighbourhood and welfare state structures (especially by the domain of the church), where support services are tied to criteria of 'morality and good behaviour' of individuals in the sense of the *Aleanza* ideology.

In this respect, it is worthwhile not only to pay attention to diverging ideological arguments, but also to concrete practice and concepts. Only in this way can breaks and continuities in comparison to the traditional concept of the Keynesian welfare state be more clearly revealed. Typically, in this context, measures which in a 'system-conformist' manner bear upon cuts (cuts of social expenditures and services), mix with those which imply 'structural reforms' in the sense of system change.

The end of social welfare as we know it

At the centre of the more recent 'social reforms' in the European Union member states stands the aspiration to restructure the social state ever more in accordance with the principle of *individual responsibility* of single individuals and to extend the duty of *individual self-provision.* Thus, the principle of collective insurance and (limited) redistribution is pushed back. The ideal that the social state has to guarantee 'inalienable claims' and the realisation of social citizens' rights is completely riddled with holes. The principle of *equality of opportunity* – which was always aimed at the elimination of the causes of social discrimination and at equal 'chances at the start' as well as post facto correction of market results reinforcing inequalities – is transformed into the principle of *justice of opportunity*. The latter sees social inequality as an indispensable and welcome catalyst for economic growth and increase in economic well-being whereby, following the principle of individual responsibility, it is only at the level of 'chances at the start' (for example education, promotion of 'employability', and so on) that state intervention could be legitimated. As the example of education and the investment in human capital shows, opportunity does not necessarily flow from social state means, but also from market stimuli and the promotion of private postgraduate training. The principle of *equality of distribution* ('policies of material equality') and the goal of producing *almost equal life conditions* must of necessity fall by the wayside in the framework of such a re-evaluation of priorities.

This fundamental reorientation can be observed – in many gradations and appearances – in the member state 'reforms' of pensions, the health systems, labour market policy and in basic social insurance (in Germany social aid). The reform of old-age insurance is inspired by the 'three-column-model' of the World Bank. In accordance with it, the public pension schemes are reduced more or less to the function of basic security in old age and supplemented by – capitalised and individualised – company pension schemes (pension funds) and voluntary private provision to make up an acceptable living standard. Pension reforms in the Netherlands and Sweden (1999), Germany (2001), Austria (2003) and France (2003, and beyond), while with different emphases, point in this direction. Moreover, they are linked closely to the intended creation of a European financial market as a key source of finance.

The reforms of public health systems, introduced or planned, have the same underlying principle: restrictive definitions of the 'medically necessary' duty to provide examinations and services, privatisation and social cut-backs by way of personal contributions, and outsourcing of the treatments and services from the state service (for example, in dental or optical treatment), private payments or supplementary insurances. In these cases, the question is primarily one of relieving businesses from 'supplementary personnel costs', which is often expressed in lower financial obligations on employers for social security systems. The general market-correcting and redistributive function of social security systems on the whole is driven backwards. A growing proportion of public services is dependent on individual 'market success' (in the case of old-age insurance, even on 'financial market success').

For unemployment insurance (long-term and youth unemployment) and basic social insurance, concepts from the USA (workfare) became and increasingly become guides to action. The concept of '*workfare*' is best expressed by the slogan 'Work for your welfare'. The Norwegian International Labour Office expert Nanna Killdal (2000) described this concept pertinently: 'Workfare programmes require benefit recipients capable of working to work for the payment they receive, but at worse conditions than those for comparable work on the "free labour market". The target group are usually not all mentally retarded recipients of state services from the basic social insurance.' The basic idea therefore is that the 'clients of the social state' have to return something to the 'community' for the receipt of a support payment in the form of low-wage labour. Workfare programmes were introduced during Ronald Reagan's administration in a number of US federal states. The true breakthrough, however, was reached by the democratic president Bill Clinton, in 1996, with the *Personal Responsibility and Work Opportunity Reconciliation Act*. In his words, the goal was 'to end welfare as we know it.' (see Hitchens 1999: 64 ff.; Platt 2004).

The US law aimed not at labour market policy, but concerned essentially social benefit-dependent groups (for instance, unemployed people, single mothers, and so on). It required work in exchange for state support services, limited the duration of benefits drastically (to a maximum of 60 months in a life-time, food stamps for only 3 months in a 36-month period, and so on) and imposed sanctions (withdrawal of benefits) when the cooperation of the recipients was deemed insufficient.[5]

In Britain (New Deal projects of the Blair government), the Netherlands, Belgium and Denmark ('active labour market policy') and in Germany (*Jobaktiv* law, Hartz reforms), this general direction has been followed in various degrees with respect to social security as well as labour market policy and unemployment support. Independent of the respective national peculiarities of these support systems, there predominates a trend to take back well established rights and claims (to 'passive support payments' as well as 'promotion' in the form of retraining, basic education and post-graduate training). Payments are tied to obligations and 'duties' (readiness to move, acceptance of precarious and low-wage jobs, work obligation for social aid recipients, and so on), and a tough regime of sanctions (partial or complete withdrawal of payments in the case of insufficient cooperation and 'fulfilment of duty') is enforced. Thus, the equal treatment clause and the old welfare state ideal of indivisible social citizenship rights are being undermined. For the lowest strata of the economically inactive (in Germany, social and unemployment benefit recipients) special legal relationships are being imposed by the authoritarian state, which attribute to the clients, depending on the case group to which they are assigned, a specific status with (limited) special rights and (extended) duties. They become second-class citizens: whereas those still gainfully employed retain, for example, the right of free choice of occupation and of workplace, these benefit recipients have to be ready for high mobility and the acceptance of 'mini-jobs' without perspective and are not allowed to make any 'mistake' – otherwise they fall through the social safety net.

What is passed off as the 'modernisation of the social state' is in reality a regression to the moralising stance of the old 'workhouse' tradition.

With respect to social insurance, it has to be noted that the self-assigned task of preventing poverty and social exclusion – or formulated in a positive manner, the securing of a socio-cultural existential minimum – does not succeed, and is not even intended, any longer. The average income from basic social security (social aid) in the 1990s in Great Britain amounted to 18%, in Portugal 22%, in France 27% in Germany 33% of the gross national income per head.

The Statistical Office of the European Union defines the poverty level as 50% of the national gross domestic product per head (see Guibentif/Bouget 1997).

Reinterpretation of the basic concepts of the social state

In parallel to the practical trials to 'modernise the social state', its central guiding concepts are being reformulated. The concept of reform in the 1970s still stood for social progress and the extension of the social state. Today those dependent on paid employment, pensioners (women and men), unemployed and social security recipients of both sexes, automatically take cover when this word is spoken.

The notion of '*solidarity*' experiences a significant change of meaning. In the context of the Keynesian welfare state ideal, it did not mean only risk sharing (social insurance), but also financing of the welfare state by all social groups according to their economic means (solidarity between economically weak and strong including businesses and the wealthy). From the tax, wage and labour policy point of view, it is now being reinterpreted into '*solidarity with the competitive*': general tax reductions with disproportionate relief of business profits, high incomes, moderation in collective agreements, firm-level flexibility (labour time, work conditions, work contract conditions) and break-up of local collective agreements are supposed to deliver higher growth and more global competitiveness, which would then stabilise the employment level and lead to falling unemployment figures in the long run. In Germany, in the meantime, even the progressive income tax is up for grabs.

Thus the White Book *Growth, Competitiveness, Employment* of the European Commission of 1993, for example, demanded a 'new social compact'. Solidarity was there defined essentially as a task to be solved between those, 'who have work, and those who have none'. The wages of those employed, in accordance with an 'insider-outsider-theory', were too high in comparison to what they would be in a labour market with perfect competition. Therefore, moderate wage increases below the growth in productivity would be required (thus wage renunciation by those employed), so that the unemployed might have the chance to get a job. A redistribution between capital and labour as the basis for solidarity is given up in favour of redistribution only between employed and unemployed ('redistribution within a class').

According to a similar pattern, old-age insurance for all is hardly a task for the whole society any longer, but a question of '*solidarity between the generations*', i.e. between the shrinking number of young gainfully employed and the growing number of older people of pension age, or rather a 'new distribution problem' derived from that between people without any children and those with many.[6] The question is thus to restrict the duty of solidarity to more narrowly defined groups and questions, with the economically strong mostly exempt. On the other hand, there are also tendencies in the socio-political debates to exclude certain risks as 'of one's own making' or to be privately borne (for example smoking, alcoholism, some kinds of sports with a high risk of accident in health insurance, incapacity for work in the case of pension insurance) from the context of solidarity.

It is no different with the concept of '*full employment*'. Following Keynes and Beveridge, it was a question of full employment on the basis of a standardised 'normal work relationship' (with regulation by collective agreement, social insurance law, and so on). Full employment was defined as a situation where the number of job vacancies, at least as a general rule, exceeded the number of those registered as unemployed. Now it is a matter of 'full employment' without standardisation of work relationships – thus under conditions of widespread precarious employment relationships (small jobs, mini-jobs, part-time, stand by, and so on) with low wages. This notion of full employment lacks the social content that was formerly present. And also from the purely quantitative point of view, it is simply attached to the achievement of a certain employment quota (share of the employed in the whole population capable of working between 14 and 65). An employment ratio of 70%, which the European Union equates to full employment, in the year 2000 in Sweden (73%) still went along with an official unemployment rate of a full 6%.

The 'crisis of the Keynesian welfare state' is thus not only interpreted differently, but the different concepts and main ideas guiding action in the quest for 'restructuring' or 'modernisation' of the social state, while similar on the surface, are based on different concepts and principles. The European Union has – due to its lack of real, independent competence in social policy – in the recent past taken on more and more the role of a 'provider of guiding images' and 'coordinator' for the social state policies of the member states.

IV
The coordination of Social Policy in the European Union: 'Social Integration', 'Pension Reforms', 'Health Care' and 'Old-Age Insurance'

Already in the 1990s, the European Commission began by trying to establish a minimum consensus between the governments of the member states concerning the 'modernisation of social protection'. It achieved this in particular by the debate on its memorandum of the same name of 1997. In 1999, there resulted the first conclusions towards a common strategy of the European Union and its member states: 'The social protection systems of the member states are faced with a number of significant common challenges. Thus, they have to be adapted, for example, to the changing world of work, new family structures and the dramatic demographic change of the upcoming decades. In this context, it is the clear wish of the citizens that the achieved high level of protection be maintained, and that it be brought into sync with the necessity to provide public services in a more efficient manner and subject them to a strict budgetary discipline. (COM 1999)'

Guiding vision: 'modernisation of social protection'

The reference to 'new family structures' is, by the way, only a mild reflection of the call for a women's policy, which in the memorandum of 1997 had still played a more prominent role: a departure from the role model of the 'male head of the household' by way of the individualisation of the tax systems and social protection (linked to a better respect for independent legal claims of women and protection of 'typically female' employment career paths with space for child rearing and care periods, and so on in the social insurances as well as an improvement of the infrastructures of care). This comparatively 'feminist' orientation was not so much due to a conscious commitment of European policy to the goals of the women's movement, but rather to economic imperatives. The goal of the Commission, to keep labour supply high in the light of demographic transformation (and to thus maintain 'competitively low' labour costs), from their point of view, could only be reached if the gainful employment quota of women, among other things, was significantly raised. Higher economic activity by women is therefore a 'means to an end' of achieving a continuously dynamic economy with high rates of economic growth.

The 'changed world of work' made it necessary that 'systems of social protection (. . .) take account of the emergence of new forms of work such as time work and part-time work, as well as the growing significance of independent entrepreneurial activity, and promote it (COM 1999).' The conclusion was: 'an adaptation to such changes requires a new balance between security and flexibility as well as between rights and duties. The systems should now offer active help to employees and job seekers, especially by way of promotion of employability and flexibility, and must create strong incentives to look for employment and to take care that work is profitable.' It is thus not a question of rolling back the devaluation of gainful employment and the increase in precarious employment. The Commission in no way seeks to establish a new European work-time standard (shortened labour-time, fully secured part-time). It is concerned with pushing on further with the flexibilisation of the labour markets and to reflect this in a downward staircase (labour law, social protection) in the restructuring of the social insurance systems. It is above all the (actual as well as potential) employed as future 'entrepreneurs of their own labour power' who have to cultivate adaptability. For this there is needed a 'new balance of rights and duties', which would encompass the workfare approach. 'Incentives' have to get the unemployed and the other 'clients' of the minimal social security systems on their toes to get a job. This is, of course, expressed in a 'friendly' or objectively-bureaucratic language, as is typical of the institutions of the European Union.

The main objective of the Commission is expressed, however, in the context of the cost question. The economy is not supposed to be burdened with too high taxes and wage supplement costs. The demographic development – that is, the expected inversion of the age pyramid with less young people gainfully employed and ever more people of pension age in a shrinking population – is mainly understood as a cost problem for the pension and health systems. This is supposed to be solved by appropriate cost cutting schemes. And above all it imposes the commandment to keep strict budgetary discipline (in accordance with the rules of the European Union Treaty and the stability and growth pact), which – given the aim of tax reductions and low wage supplementary costs – means to limit and drive back state financing of social security systems.

The 'over-ageing of the population': Can we no longer afford the social state?

In the perception of the Commission and the governments of the member states, we apparently have to deal with a 'demographic time-bomb'. Between 2000 and 2050 the old-age coefficient (the relationship between people of employment age between 15 and 64 years to people of pension age over 65) is supposed to almost double, from 28.3% to 55.9% in the EU-15 average. Put another way: at this point, on average 3.5 gainfully employed people are available to support one pensioner; in the year 2050 there are only supposed to be 1.8 gainfully employed persons. Expenditure on pensions at this time in the EU-average run at about 12% of the European Union's gross domestic product (for the health systems it is 7%). Pension expenditures are set to grow in a number of member states, up to 15 to 20% of their national GDP. This, say the Commission, governments, employers' associations, experts and media, simply cannot be accomplished – the social security systems can no longer continue to be financed in this way.

In practice, the problem could be even worse. Because the old-age coefficient expresses only the relationship between gainfully employable people and those of pension age. But not all of those who are gainfully employable actually have a job. In 2003, the employment quota (the share of people of gainfully employable age, who actually have a gainful job) was on average 64%. If this were still the situation in 2050, there would only be 1.15 gainfully employed for one pensioner. Therefore, argues the Commission, it is necessary to mobilise all possibilities (women, immigrants, the elderly employed, the prolongation of working life) to increase the employment quota and improve this ratio. What this could bring about is shown by a small model computation by Schani Margulies for Austria. In 1996, there were in Austria 1.6 million citizens (women and men) over 60 years as well as 5 million between 15 and 60 years. Of the latter, only 3.3 million were gainfully employed (employment quota of 69%). Government estimates predicted a decrease of the population in employable age (15-60) to 4.5 million by 2030. If, however, Austria succeeded in reaching an employment quota of 90% by that time, there would exist in comparison to 1996 a further 700,000 gainfully employed and 1 million more pensioners. 'Full employment' would thus significantly alleviate the demographic problem.

This is also illustrated by an examination on the basis of the German example. After all, those who are employable not only have to take care of elderly people, but also children and young people. Therefore, the overall quotient (elderly and young) is more relevant to the true 'burden' caused by the care for the economically inactive parts of the population for the employable. This overall quotient does not rise dramatically even in the projections of the Federal Statistical Office: compared to the situation in 1970 (with 'full employment and a social state intact'), in 2050 it would only be 12% higher. This is in no way dramatic, because the wealth of society increases at a much higher rate.

Table 5: Prognosis for the change in the overall quotient (young and old) for Germany

For 100 people of middle age there are

	Older	Younger	Overall	Definition of middle age
1970	40	60	100	20 to under 60
2001	44	38	82	20 to under 60
2050 a	78	34	112	20 to under 60
2050 b	55	30	85	20 to under **65**

Source: Federal Statistical Office, German Population until 2050, 10th coordinated projection, Variant 5 ('middle variant'), press release of 6/6/2003

More important insights, however, can be won from a more long-term examination of the 'demographic problem'. Today's debate is a strong reminder of the core argument of Parson Malthus, only in reverse. In 1798, at the beginning of the industrialisation period, the British economist Malthus argued that Britain in the long term could only expect poverty and famine. The population would grow geometrically, but the opening up of new agricultural space, by contrast, at best arithmetically. In a few decades, it would therefore necessarily be the case that agriculture would no longer be able to feed the dramatically increased population.

As we know today, Malthus was wrong about the 'demographic problem' back then – interpreting it as overpopulation. In the year 1800, about 75% of the West European population were employed in agriculture; in the year 2000, it is about 4-5%. In the meantime, there was a continuous development in productivity. It enabled one person employed in agriculture to provide food for about 88 persons, instead of in the beginning (1800) for only 1.4 persons. In these 200 years, overall economic productivity on average grew by 'only' 1.7% a year. Similar shifts in scale also occurred in the area of services and production. The real gross domestic product in West Germany rose by 473% between 1950 and 1990, while the number of employed in the same period rose only by 42%. Demographic development was therefore responsible for 9% of the production increase in this period; the remaining 91% was due to the growth of real capital stock, labour productivity, and so on. The central question is therefore not the relationship of the gainfully employable to pensioners (and not even of the actually economically active to the economically inactive). The question is rather, whether the progress in productivity in the future can still be as high as it was during the last 200 years to guarantee a sufficient additional product, given a relative decrease in employment. In the economies of the industrialised countries (Organisation for Economic Cooperation and Development), even with flat economic growth rates, a corresponding yearly increase in productivity of 1.5 to 1.7% for the next economic decades is expected. In this case, the maintenance and design of the social security systems in the context of an ageing and shrinking overall population is not a demographical problem, but one of *distribution*.

In a historical perspective our present demographic problem is rather modest. In Germany, the old-age coefficient in 1900 was 12.4. It sank to 6.9 in 1950, and to 4.1. in 2000. From a full 12 gainfully employable persons per pensioner down to 4 per pensioner in 100 years is surely a much more dramatic decrease than from 4 (2000) to 2 in the next 50 years (prognosis for 2050). Nonetheless, in this period living standards rose significantly and the social state was built up and extended, in particular between 1950 to 1970. After 2040, however, a stabilisation of the age structure is expected – thus, in essence, only the consequences of the ageing of the 'baby-boom' generation (those born during the 1950s and the early 1960s) have to be 'managed'.

Ageing in Germany 1871-2050

for one person over 65, there are . . . 15-65 year-old

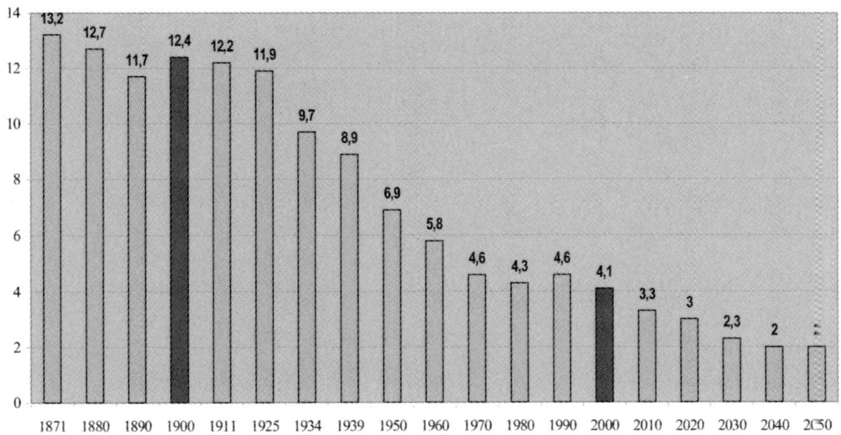

The longest stretch of the 'burden' caused by demographic change is already behind us. An 'objective need' for cost reduction for demographic reasons, as claimed by the European Commission and the governments of the member states, simply does not exist.

The European Union strategy for social integration

In the framework of the 'Lisbon strategy' – that is, its concept 'of a political triangle, which would rely on a positive mutual influence between economic, employment and social protection policy', and its goal of turning Europe into the most strongly growing and competitive knowledge-based economy of the world by the year 2010 – the European Union, has initiated in the area of social policy a number of coordination processes between the member states. These concentrate at this point on the fight against poverty and social exclusion, a coordination of pension reforms, and coordination concerning the health system and care for the elderly.

At the Nice summit (December 2000), the goals of 'open coordination' in the area of *poverty and social exclusion* were established. There are four basic orientations:

1. promotion of participation in gainful employment and access of all to resources, rights, goods and services,
2. avoidance of risks of exclusion,
3. measures in favour of the socially most endangered persons,
4. mobilising of everyone.

These orientations are obviously formulated in very vague terms. Although the preceding Portuguese Council presidency had pushed for quantifiable goals, for instance, the overcoming of child poverty by 2010, even the partial goals were formulated in a very vague manner which is open to interpretation. Thus, one of the three partial aims of Goal 2 concerns 'Measures for the Maintenance of Solidarity in the Family in all its Forms'. Under Goal 3 one finds the 'Elaboration of extensive measures for areas which are confronted with problems of exclusion.'

Moreover, despite a different definition of the method of open coordination (MOC) in the guidelines of the Council of Lisbon, the Council renounced the laying down of guidelines itself. The member states were supposed to draw up *national action plans for social inclusion* of a two year duration on the basis of the above-mentioned orientations and in this context to set themselves national goals and measures. Thus, the first round of national action plans (period of action 2001-2003) in most cases amounted to little more than a list of national problem areas and the already operational measures of the governments. Only a few set themselves concrete and binding independent goals for the prevention of poverty and social exclusion. In their draft report on the evaluation of national action plans, the European Commission expressed appropriate criticism and drew up a ranking of member states. In the joint report with the Council, this criticism and the 'ranking' was withdrawn. The Commission then pointed out that it was not its goal to evaluate the policies of the member states and their effectiveness. But this had been specifically intended in the original concept of the 'method of open coordination'.

The European Anti-Poverty Network (EAPN) concluded after this first round (2001-2003) that in less than half of the countries adequate measures were being implemented or planned to effectively address the problem of poverty and social exclusion. The members with adequate measures are for the most part countries with developed social systems, which already show a lower poverty rate. Yet even in these countries, there remain doubts as to the financial appropriateness and the quality of execution. The great majority of member states see integration into the labour market (with sanction-proven methods of 'activating labour market policy') as the most weighty instrument for the fight against poverty and social exclusion. The themes of 'poverty despite work' and of immaterial factors of social exclusion (discrimination, and so on) hardly play a role.

Key indicators were agreed upon, which are supposed to make possible an all-European comparability and control of the effectiveness of the measures by the member states: income distribution, poverty rate, entrenched poverty, share of unemployed households, regional differences in the unemployment rate, educational deficiencies and long-term unemployment. The Belgian Council presidency, in 2001, had presented proposals from expert circles, which wanted to express more broadly the defined aspects of social exclusion by using indicators: preventive health care, living situation and homelessness, language and basic mathematical skills, access to basic public services, debts, access to telecommunication and the Internet, access to social security and social insurance, participation in public life, in leisure and culture. But these proposals were rejected.

The second round of national action plans (2003-2005) has also been sharply criticised by the European Anti-Poverty Network. As before, there was no adequate anchoring of the fight against poverty and social exclusion as a cross-sectional task for all policy areas of the member states. There was a particular lack of decisive efforts to make social safety nets 'poverty-resistant', as well as of clear strategies in the various areas and of adequate equipment with financial and personnel resources. The fight against poverty and social exclusion in the meantime in most member states had an even lower priority than two years earlier. The national action plans continued to have the character of analysis and reports. The governments were, in this context, using the opportunity to publicise show projects. Policies that had increased problems of poverty, were, on the contrary, simply not mentioned.

The ten new member states of the Union have each of them concluded agreements with the European Commission (Joint Inclusion Memorandum) to prepare for a 'method of open coordination' for social integration. This concerns the build-up of capacities in the administrations dealing with these topics and their cooperation with civil society actors (non-governmental organisations, collective agreement partners, welfare associations). Often, there first has to be an inventory made of the trends in poverty and social exclusion, their origins and long-term effects, and a statistical system conforming with that of the rest of the European Union in this area. After May 2004, they are also supposed to draw up their first national action plans.

On the whole, the balance of this first coordination process of social policy looks meagre. Already in 1996, 18% of the European Union population lived in poverty (with less than 60% of the average income). In Britain, it was as much as 20%, and in Portugal 24%. Around 40% of the income-poor population (25 million citizens, male and female, of the EU 15) live in long-term poverty. Even a stable job today no longer protects against poverty. On average in the European Union, 13% of all households with at least one gainfully employed person in the family are poor. This situation has practically not changed at all. Since concrete and binding goals are being renounced at the European level, it can hardly be expected that the member states will feel compelled to make stronger efforts.

The coordination of pension reforms in the European Union

The second social policy coordination process deals with pension systems. Already in 1999, the Commission had, in a study of pension systems and public budgets, voiced the fear that some member states would be driven into increased public indebtedness to finance their pension systems. Such a development had to be avoided, since otherwise the stability of the euro and the deficit rules of the European Union treaty would be threatened. The main motivation of the open coordination concerning pension systems, which was introduced at the Stockholm summit of 2001, was thus of a fiscal nature. The Lisbon summit established three principles and eleven goals for the 'method of open coordination' for pension systems. The member states were to present in their national strategy reports how the national state pension policy follows these principles and goals. Thus, the open coordination of pension systems is also non-binding in character, in a similar way to the one concerning poverty and social exclusion.

Table 4: Principles and goals of open coordination (MOC) concerning 'Pensions which are adequate and secure into the future'

	European Goals
	A: **Adequateness of pensions**
1	Prevent social exclusion
2	Put people in a position to maintain their standard of living
3	Promotion of solidarity (among the elderly, between the generations)
	B: **Financial tolerability**
4	Raise the employment level
5	Prolong life-time work-time
6	Give pensions a secure future through the framework of solid public finances
7	Adapt services and contributions in a balanced way
8	Make sure that private old-age provision is appropriately and soundly financed
	C: **Modernisation: React to changes in needs**
9	Adapt to more flexible employment and career patterns
10	Follow the aspirations to equal status of men and women
11	Prove the capability of the pension systems to live up to the challenges

The cooperation of the member states departs from a 'three-pillar-structure' of old-age insurance as the ideal model: state pension systems, company pension systems, and voluntary private provision. The report of the Commission and Council of 2003, analysing the national strategy reports of the member states, draws the following conclusion: 'All member states have introduced the reform process and quite a few have already, in the 1990s, implemented far-reaching, in some cases even radical, reform. Nonetheless, the majority of the countries see the need for further reforms in order to secure the further tolerability of the pension systems and the solidity of public finances. (. . .) Especially important in this respect will be – in particular with a view to the long-term consequences of higher life-expectancy for pension expenditure – to create stronger incentives for older employed people to prolong their working lives. This can be attained mainly by a closer connection between contributions and payments. Beyond that, the financial basis of the pension systems can be strengthened by the extension of state and private capital funding.'

The Barcelona summit (2002) had already agreed upon a retreat from the policy of early pensions and established a target for older employees: until 2010, the *real* average age at which the gainfully employed retire should be raised gradually by five years. In many member states, a considerable proportion of employees quit working before reaching the legal pension age. This development should be resisted by way of 'incentives' (cuts in case of premature entry into pension; flexible work-time; opposition to age discrimination in the labour-market) and thus prolonging actual working life.

The European Union is not able to judge in a well-founded way whether pension incomes (from all three pillars) are 'adequate' to ultimately secure pensioners' living standards. The data in the national strategy reports 'allow no systematic comparison of the present and future replacement quota levels (that is the ratio of former employment income to pension; *A.B.*) in the members states.' The report of the Commission and Council, moreover, states simply that pensions in general are 'appropriate'; however, concrete numbers are only provided for those at risk of poverty in the population who are aged over 65 years. For pensioners in general, this was not higher than for the rest of the population; however, for the female aged population, it is considerably higher. What follows from taking the 'reform course' in the direction of cost cutting and partial privatisation is revealed by a very few indications in the report: 'Belgium and Italy call the differences in income between pensioner households continuously worrisome. Italy declares that income differentials are the highest between the younger pensioners, which reflects the growing importance of company pensions (which have a less pronounced redistributive character) and income from other sources (especially capital returns) in this age group. In the report from the United Kingdom, it is stated that the income of the 20% highest pension recipients from 1979 to 1996/7 increased by 80%, whilst that of the 20% lowest pension recipients rose only by 30%. This is to be attributed to the extension of the individual and company-level old-age provision, a trend which does not benefit the poorest pensioners.'

It also seems difficult to make well-grounded statements about the *future* 'appropriateness' of pensions. Pensions from state systems will be limited and tend to be cut back to the level of 'social basic insurance'. The second and third pillars should then in theory help to secure the living standard. However, they are increasingly switched to individual capital funds. Thus, the pension system as a whole acts in a less redistributive fashion, and the future level of payments depends increasingly on the success of investments in the financial markets and the respective moment the payment comes due. In the Netherlands, Britain and Germany, pension funds and life insurance concerns – the suppliers of the capital-funded pillar – have got into deep water. Maybe this also led to state intervention with tax subsidies (so that the claimed 'relief of the public budgets' is also questionable).[7]

The principles and goals of open coordination in the pension area, though they at first sight often sound well, are actually more an Orwellian 'newspeak' aimed at assuaging public opinion: 'Trust us, it will all end well, socially and in a solidarity-based fashion!' The message to tomorrow's pensioners, which the German economic wise man Horst Siebert has formulated, on the other hand, describes the 'reform course' with refreshing openness and realism: 'Work longer, own less, save more!'

The European Union guideline concerning company pensions (2003)

Largely unnoticed by the political public, the European Union passed, in Spring 2003, a new legal regulation concerning company pension systems. Typically, it is a guideline in the framework of the financial market action plan, which is aimed at the creation of the integrated financial market in the European Union. In the case of company pensions, employers and employees usually contribute to a savings fund, from which the employees later receive pension benefits. Such systems can be set up by the business itself or they can use the services of another financial institution (e.g. pension funds, pension insurance or investment funds). This then receives the contributions, invests them and pays out the retirement pensions. Business pension systems in the European Union currently hold assets corresponding to about 29% of the gross domestic product of the European Union (2.5 trillion). If this area – which is regulated in many various ways by the national states – were to be opened up to competition and deregulated, truly European pensions funds could develop. This is a goal of the European Union guideline 'About the activity of institutions for company pension provision' that was passed.

It opens the rendering of services for company pension systems to a European Union-wide competition and liberalises the investment rules. The management of the asset and investment values of firm-based pension schemes, in the future, should be based on the *prudent person principle* . According to this principle, the contributions made should be invested in the best possible interest of the members. The financial administration and investment strategy should be transparent and carried out by qualified financial mangers. These and certain reserve provisions should suffice to keep a 'sensible balance' between investment risk and security of pension payments. Members and beneficiaries of the company pension systems have to be correctly informed about the conditions of the system, their individual rights and payment claims, investment strategy and the financial position of the supplier.

Beyond that, the guideline makes no stipulations concerning the security of pension payments: neither does the later payment have to correspond at least to the sum of the money invested, nor does it have to guarantee a minimal return. In other respects as well, the stipulations offer financial managers considerable freedom of movement; the future company pensions can either be paid out for life, or only over an agreed period, or as a one-time payment. They can cover biometric risks (invalidity, high age) and the care of dependents, but in that case higher contributions can be demanded.

The contributions (i.e. the portfolio) can be invested up to 70% in stocks and other obligations, up to 30% also in foreign currencies. An engagement in risky capital markets is explicitly allowed. A number of member countries up to now had stricter quantitative and qualitative investment prescriptions. The suppliers of services (pensions and investment funds, life insurances, and so on) in the future will be allowed to manage business pension systems in all member states. However, they have to respect the other investment provisions of the national state of the respective member states and their tax, social and labour law prescriptions. Thus, the creation of European pension funds is made possible, but the conditions of their operation are not yet completely harmonised across the European Union.

The argument of the Commission for the European Union business pension guideline announces in surprising clarity what the real issues of pension reform and the strengthening of capital-funded old-age provision really are: 'The establishments for business old-age provision distinguish themselves by their very long-term activities with respect to the commitments of the carrying business as well as by their investments (...) Therefore, they can, if they hold this to be appropriate from the point of view of the kind and duration of their portfolio, effect substantial investments into relatively illiquid assets, such as stocks, including those issued by very small firms, yes, even into unquoted securities. In this way, the establishments (. . .) can make a contribution to the development of risk capital. With a view to the better spread of their investment portfolio, they can also invest significant sums in foreign securities. (. . .) The institutions of company-level old-age provision thus play an important role in the national systems of social security, in the financing of the European Union economy, and in the integration of the European capital markets. (. . .) The institutions for company-level pensions invest increasingly in stocks and shares, which in the long run are seen as more profitable and thereby contribute to a reinforced capitalisation of the stock markets of the member states, which continues to constitute only around half of that of the US.'[8] Pension funds can act like major banks as credit and capital providers for new firms and established enterprises. Europe-wide pension funds would reduce the financing and administrative costs of the insurance industries due to economies of scale. Old-age security increasingly becomes the play money of finance, which expects good business from it. This in turn strengthens the strategy of increasing 'shareholder value' and the dominance of financial markets. Both find in the European Commission and in governments of the member states all too willing helpers.

Coordination for the future of the health system and long-term care

The third process of social policy coordination in the European Union deals with the future of the health system and old-age care. The Barcelona summit (2002) initiated an open coordination on this topic on the basis of a memorandum by the Commission of 2001.

The Commission had formulated three European Union-wide goals to be pursued:

- access for each and everyone independent of their income or wealth
- a high level of quality of the health systems and care for the elderly
- securing the financial solvency of the systems.

The member states were asked to prepare a questionnaire about the national situation and strategies in these three areas. On this basis, there took shape in spring 2003 the first joint report of Commission and Council concerning the national strategies in the area of the health system and old-age care. Whereas the Commission emphasised very strongly the cost implications of demographic change in this area, the Common Report expresses itself more cautiously in this respect. Overall, the Common Report comes out with much less detail than, for example, the reports about social integration or the pension systems. It concedes that there were certainly problems with respect to equal access to health and old-age care (especially for elderly people and people with low income; regional differences in provision, waiting periods for certain treatments, and so on). In most member states, the households bore between 20-30% of the overall health costs, either directly or by way of private additional insurances. Legal limitations on the service that is available, additional payments and self-payment regulations are common. This situation created risks that the 'vulnerable groups would not be in a position to afford such expenditures and would therefore either not want or not be able to permit themselves appropriate basic care.'

With respect to the guarantee of a high quality of provision, standards for structural quality (medical equipment, qualification and post-graduate training of personnel, buildings and installation standards) were in the meantime usually available. The situation was more difficult as far as process quality (treatment guidelines, and so on) was concerned. The evaluation of services and results of the health systems and old-age care was systematically undertaken only in a few member states.

With respect to financing the systems, it is claimed that in some member states since the end of the 1990s, health expenditures were growing faster than gross domestic product. The short-term reactions of the member states were very different one from the other. Some had stabilised their level of expenditures and saw no immediate need for consolidation (for example, Spain). Others were taking measures to channel more resources into the health system (for example, Denmark, Britain). And a third group would fight to avoid rising expenditures (e.g. Germany and France). The long-term prognoses concerning expenditure increases on the basis of demographic change and expensive medical-technical progress rely essentially on a study of the Economic Policy Committee of the European Union (2001). It works on the assumption of a rise in health expenditures in the course of the next 50 years (2000-2050) between 0.7 and 2.3% of GDP. The report cautions, however, that these prognoses on the basis of the underlying assumptions were to be treated 'with caution'.[9] Even if they applied, it is not a question of an insurmountable challenge.

In contrast to the coordination processes for social integration and the pension reforms, the production of European 'models' in the area of health care and care for old people has not advanced much. Indicators and guidelines are not yet in existence. At this time, it is still the member states – see the German 'health structure reform' and the debate about the 'head tax' by the Herzog Commission – which sethe course of system change. However, it should not be underestimated that the Commission (also in the framework of the 'economic policy guidelines', the stability and growth pact and its forays into the liberalisation of the sectors of public provision and services) targets the state-organised health systems and social insurances and includes them in the computation of the public deficit quotas. The industrial lobby has for a long time run a campaign for a European domestic market in health services and products, which is bound to result in the liberalisation and privatisation of the health sector and care for the elderly.

The European Commission in its Memorandum of 2001 clearly points at its competence with respect to the application of the principles of the domestic market in the area of health provision (patient mobility, liberalisation of services). It points out that, following Article 85 and 86 of the European Union Treaty, health insurances and the institutions charged with the administration of systems of social security fulfil a task of solely social state character only, if their activity is based on the principle of national solidarity and is not aimed at making profit. To be able to do so, the relevant services have to be legally enshrined and be independent of the level of contributions paid. The new guideline draft of the Commission for the creation of a *domestic market* for services up to 2010 also concerns the professions in the health system as well as the system itself.

The consequences are unmistakable: 'should the European market and competition law assert itself more forcefully as a result of the new coordination method, this would lead to a deregulation of the whole system of contracts and services. If the health insurances were understood in the sense of the European competition law as economic enterprises, all contracts with hospital boards, doctors' associations and the other care providers would be evaluated as collusion contrary to competition. They would lose their validity and everything would have to be steered by market relationships. If then on top of that is added the primacy of cost reduction and privatisation from the euro financial regime, this would strengthen those political forces which have always wanted to deform the health system by the introduction of more market competition, and the narrowing of service provision.' (Urban 2003).

V
The Lisbon Strategy and competition-oriented embedding of social policy: a new European social model?

The Lisbon strategy already mentioned several times aims to reconcile economic, employment and social policy with one another. Since the Lisbon summit (2000), the spring session of the European Council is therefore regularly devoted to these economic and social questions and prepared by a 'synthetic report' from the European Commission. Thus a multitude of coordination processes at the European Union level are included in the examination, which are partly listed in the European Union Treaty and partly rely on the *method of open coordination*.

Economic policy coordination

The European Union economic policy in the Treaty is determined as a 'matter of common interest' and should therefore be coordinated in the Council. According to Article 4 of the Treaty, it has to pursue the following landmark principles: 'Stable prices, sound public finances and monetary conditions as well as a permanently sustainable balance of payments.' (The Federal German Stability Law of 1967, by contrast, also included goals of full employment and economic growth.) With the Stability and Growth Pact (Council resolution of December 13, 1997 and Guideline 1466/97), the Protocol over the procedure in case of excessive deficit and the provisions of the EU Treaty (Article 104 ECT), there exists a solid framework for the coordination of the budgetary policies of the member states. They are supposed to keep their budgetary deficits below 3% of their gross domestic product (GDP), and the overall state debt is not supposed to exceed 60% of the respective GDP. Going far beyond that, the member states had committed themselves to reach balanced budgets by 2004 and even to achieve budget surpluses. As soon as the budgetary situation in one member state departs strongly from the agreed goals, the Council can, upon a proposal by the Commission with a qualified majority, address a recommendation to the member state concerned – the dreaded 'warning letter' from Brussels, which up to now has been issued to Portugal, France, and Germany.

Coordination of the economic policies of the member states takes place by way of annual Guidelines ('Basic guidelines of economic policy') with recommendations for the European Union and for each single member state. The main points of emphasis are, as before, price stability and budgetary consolidation. Since 1998, however, the following themes have also been added: structural reforms of the goods and capital markets (liberalisation policy), the flexibilisation of the labour market, as well as more efficient and better integrated financial markets. Inasmuch as the economic policy of a member state grossly contradicts these guidelines or threatens the functioning of the currency union, the Council can, by qualified majority, also address a recommendation to the state concerned. This was done in 2001 in the case of Ireland, because the overheated economic growth there, in the eyes of the other member states, threatened the inflationary goal of the European Central Bank. The European Parliament on its own initiative set up a report concerning the economic policy guidelines. Formally, it has in that respect no co-deliberation rights – the Council merely informs it of its decision.

The contractual corset for the economic policy of the European Union is unambiguously monetarist in nature – at the centre, there are low inflation rates and debt reduction. Added to that are policies for the shaping and deepening of the European domestic market. That is mainly the issue in the so-called Cardiff process (1998). Its goals are 'Structural Reforms in the EU Domestic Market': a higher flexibility of goods and capital markets, the integration of European financial markets, the coordination of labour market and financial reforms, the fight against state subsidies, the prevention of unlawful tax competition, as well as deepening and extending the reach of comprehensive liberalisation projects, which were begun in the framework of the domestic market (e.g. energy, telecommunications, railways, postal services, public tenders, and so on). It delivers important substantive preparatory work for the economic policy guidelines and the prescriptive goals of the domestic market strategy.

The European Union summits in Göteburg and Stockholm have, moreover, set their sights on the 'environmental dimension of the Community'. It is supposed to be taken into account by way of a 'strategy for sustainable development' in the framework of the Lisbon strategy, with a view to climate change, transport, public health and natural resources. This does not entail a coordination of the environmental policies of the member states, but an investigation of the effects of European Union policies (agrarian and structural policies, transport and trans-European networks, and so on) on the achievement of 'sustainability goals'. Up to now, the 'sustainability dimension' has found its expression essentially by the inclusion of a corresponding paragraph in the economic policy guidelines, which bears primarily upon market economic instruments, for example for reaching the Kyoto climate protection goals.

The European employment strategy

On the basis of Article 128 ECT, a coordinated EU employment strategy with annual European guidelines has evolved – the so-called Luxemburg process (1997). The member states implement these guidelines in National Action Plans for employment policy. The guidelines in the past were grouped around four themes: equal opportunities for women and men, improvement of employability, development of the entrepreneurial spirit and job creation, promotion of adaptability of businesses and their employees. They have a low degree of binding commitment and are subordinated to the goals of economic policy guidelines. In addition, Article 125 EC Treaty limits 'employment policy' in the main to labour market policy and labour market reforms for more flexible labour markets. The Parliament is formally consulted when the employment political guidelines are drawn up; that means it can make a statement before the Council finally decides.

The social policy side of the Lisbon strategy is covered by the open coordination processes concerning social inclusion, pensions, health and care for the elderly (see part IV).

The tightening of the economic, social, and employment policy coordination processes in the European Union (since 2003)

The coordination processes concerning economic, employment, social and environmental policies in the European Union were relatively divided as well as, from the point of view of content and time, hardly in sync with each other. Commission and Council wanted to remedy this by a temporal synchronisation as well as thematic bundling and tightening. Since 2003, the *economic policy guidelines* , the *domestic market strategy*, and the *employment policy guidelines* are being set up to the same rhythm. This gives rise to the following timetable: in January, the Commission presents a comprehensive report, which includes the implementation report for the economic policy guidelines, the draft of the common employment report, and the implementation report for the domestic market strategy, the stability and convergence programmes, the Cardiff report and a few other reports of the Commission, for example, on state subsidies. At the same time, the Commission presents its Spring report concerning the Lisbon strategy, where the most important aspects and strategic policy priorities are put together. These two reports, together with the subject papers from councillors containing important demands for the respective policy areas, are presented to the European Council in March.

After the European Council has controlled the realisation and put forward general political orientations, the Commission in April presents its proposals for further progress in the named policy areas. This guiding package contains the economic as well as the employment political guidelines. Given the desired long-term horizon, this package covers a temporal span of three years (at present 2003-2006) and is only adapted in the case of important new developments in the meantime. After further deliberations of the European Parliament (concerning the employment political guidelines) and the responsible ministerial councils of the subject areas, the European Parliament will approve the guidelines at its regular meeting in June.

The better to guarantee implementation, the Commission relies upon an improved national report system, for example, fewer, but more comprehensible and precise reports. These are supposed to be presented by October. On this basis, but also on the basis of bilateral contacts and results of benchmark comparisons, the Commission weighs the successes in realisation and presents its results in a new implementation report in mid-January, when a new cycle begins.

As far as *substantial coordination* is concerned, the basic features of economic policy (as the 'big guidelines') continue to remain at the centre. They will, however, be more strategically aligned, with an emphasis on macroeconomics, economic structural reforms (liberalisation, integration of financial markets), and measures for the promotion of growth, employment, social cohesion, and sustainable development. The employment policy guidelines are simplified and expressed more briefly. The domestic market strategy is elaborated in more detail. The Commission proposes, moreover, to supplement this tightening of the coordination processes after 2006 by a comprehensive strategy in the area of social protection (2006-2009, that means in time for the next 'synchronisation period'). This would then include the areas of social integration, pensions as well as health care provision and care for the elderly, which would then be brought together in 'a common report concerning social protection' and be put into operation by way of national strategy reports and all-European goals.

The leading function of economic policy guidelines is unchanged

No doubt it is necessary to join up and tighten the multitude of coordination processes. While the rhetoric of the Lisbon strategy has, up to now, followed a balanced treatment of economic, employment, and social policy as well as environmental sustainability, and demanded work on the conflicting goals of the various endeavours, the current narrowing reinforces the already existing hierarchies in the policy fields. The 'economic policy guidelines' clearly dominate, as is underlined by the incorporation of social, employment and environmental policy declarations into the guidelines. Economic policy guidelines and domestic market strategy together give the closer coordination a bias in the direction of strict budgetary discipline and cost-cutting, as well as liberalisation and flexibilisation. Political guidelines on employment and social protection have to support this framework and become subordinate to it.

In the economic policy guidelines 2003, it becomes obvious: 'The basic features (of economic policy; *A.B.*) stand at the centre of the efforts for policy coordination, which characterises the system of economic policy leadership in the European Union and its member states. Through these basic tenets, the European Union expresses the belief that higher and sustainable growth rates are of decisive importance and that it is resolutely decided to take the measures necessary for their achievement. To increase economic welfare in a sustainable way, sound macroeconomic conditions are needed, and a solid macroeconomic policy. A stronger entrepreneurial spirit and higher investments in knowledge and innovation are of central significance for new growth opportunities. Better functioning and more compatible labour, product, and capital markets are indispensable to achieving a more flexible economy and increase potential growth. (. . .) In particular, wages should, in the case of a possible cyclical recovery of productivity or of an inflationary push due to oil price rises, continue to grow moderately, so that profit margins may recover further and thus favour investment growth leading to job creation.'

The Guidelines contain an 'explanation' of unemployment in the European Union which takes one's breath away: 'That the per capita gross domestic product (of the European Union; *A.B.*) lies well below the US level is explained mainly by the fact that fewer persons have a job and tend to work fewer hours. This may in part be attributable to the fact that leisure time is accorded a higher status; in many cases, however, it can be reduced to the simple question, *whether work is worth it*? (emphasis in the original; *A.B.*). By way of relatively generous or rather liberal social protection systems or through early retirement incentives, many people were effectively encouraged to leave the labour market or to remain unemployed.' The social state is thus to blame for the high unemployment. Thus it has to be 'modernised', and labour markets have to be freed of regulations.

In what follows, one finds recommendations that the European Union summit in Barcelona in 2002 had already urged. Wages had to be more strongly differentiated according to productivity and qualification (that means, mainly, to be reduced even further in the lower income brackets). Furthermore, 'the costs in connection with the formulation of labour contracts and their termination' should be re-examined. In plain text: a flexibilisation of labour contract law and, for example, the weakening of protection against dismissal were demanded.

Claims for benefits, their duration, compensation for lost wages and supplementary payments, and so on under unemployment insurance are required to be re-examined and tied to sharper obligations. In this respect, the employment policy guidelines of 2003 send the same clear message to the member states: 'they will, in particular, under maintenance of an appropriate level of social protection, control the wage replacement quotas and the duration of receipt of benefit, they will, taking into account the individual situation, guarantee an effective administration of payments, in particular with respect to tying them to effective job search, including access to active help for the improvement of individual placement chances; they will, if need be, consider the granting of wage replacement benefits and strive for the elimination of benefit traps. Measures will be aimed in particular at substantially lowering, by 2010, the high effective marginal tax rates and, if need be, the tax and supplement burden on the wages of low-wage earners in relation to national conditions.'

Thus the fight against poverty and social exclusion is then seen essentially from the point of view that more flexible labour markets and more availability of mini-jobs and low wage employment offer the best protection against their spread: 'important in particular are measures that will improve the functioning of the labour markets and are conceived such that the wages reflect productivity differences in the various trades and local labour market conditions.' (BEPG 2003).

The reforms of the pension and health systems are addressed: 'the requirement to insure the long-term sustainability of public finances has been underscored by the European Councils in Lisbon, Stockholm, and Barcelona. To deal with the economic and budgetary impact of the ageing of the population, the European Council in Stockholm decided to pursue a three-pronged strategy. The main emphasis of this strategy should lie in the strengthening of the gainful employment quota (see part II), the lowering of state debt, as well as on the reform of pension and health systems (BEPG).' As a central orientation for pension systems there is offered the prolongation of life-time employment, the achievement of financial sustainability, and the extension of 'additional pension provision systems'.

The employment policy guidelines (and future declarations concerning social protection) have to follow the tenets of the economic policy guidelines. The latter, however, already include an ensemble of economic and social policy statements, which can hardly be 'mitigated' and even less corrected by other political strategies and points of emphases. The tightening up and synchronisation of the Lisbon strategy in fact achieves the production of a coherence between economic, employment and social policy: the social state is being demolished.

A new European social model?

Social protection in Europe has always been understood as a 'productive factor'. The prevention of accidents by way of measures for health and safety protection at the workplace, an efficient health system, state educational policy and active labour market policy (retraining, qualification, post-graduate education) have also strengthened the productivity of businesses.

While in the Keynesian welfare state this was partially linked to the social character of wage labour, social policy now is supposed to become a much more immediate factor for improved international competitiveness: 'Gradually, at the level of the national state as well as on the European plane, the contours of a New European Social Model are becoming visible, and on all fours with the competitive political formation of the economic space of Europe in the sense of the Lisbon strategy. In this model, a social policy continues. However, it is one which will no longer contribute much to the securing of the social rights of citizens (women and men) and to protection against the impositions of the capitalist market economy. In this New European Social Model, social policy gradually becomes a variant of competitiveness policy. The social policy programmes of the European Union aim above all at the improvement of the supply conditions of businesses, for example by way of the increase in the qualification and the health status of the employees or the quick placement of the unemployed. It is above all a matter of enterprise competitiveness and economy-wide value creation.' (Urban 2003).

The 'New European Social Model' exists predominantly as a European guideline – as a blueprint, which is being implemented by the nation states in accordance with different historical traditions and social relationships of forces. The already severely hit Keynesian welfare state is being closed down on the basis of the developments introduced by the neoliberal revolution. While the guiding ideas of 'modernising the social state' are the same all over Europe, the implementation should bring with it not only convergence, but also still further differentiation of the national 'social states'. Their 'implementation' by the national states is still mostly tied in to the national welfare state traditions, as they have developed historically. New 'systems' logics' (capital-coverage principle for pensions, liberalisation and competition in health care and long-term care, private job placement, and so on) are intertwined with the cut-back remnants of the old structures.

On the one hand, we witness more and more a social protection riddled with holes, as we already know it from the *liberal welfare state*. Yet, the 'modernisation of the social state' clearly goes beyond the traditional liberal model. Where Beveridge still saw minimum social protection as a legal claim of individuals to secure a dignified existence, today there rules more and more the spirit of the workhouse charged with moralising imperatives of duty and punishment. The partial privatisation and individualisation of the pension system turns the previous 'solidarity-based system' into a vehicle for speculation and gaming on the financial markets. The health system is steered increasingly by the imperatives of competition.

While the social state (and even more so the extended Keynesian welfare state) formerly put reins on capitalism, in order to protect it against itself, the film is now being rewound: the complete unleashing of market forces, and this with the support of state social policy. The uncertain European public will probably still need a while, until it grasps what historical performance it is being offered here in the name of the New Europe.

Notes

1 Some authors already see the introduction of the European Currency System (ECS) in 1979 as a precursor of this development. Compare Beckmann/Bieling/Deppe 2003.

2 At this point, I cannot answer the question to what extent the social security systems of the member states can be evaluated according to the categories of the four welfare state models by Esping-Andersen. This can be tried by professionally more involved social and political scientists.

3 The early enlightenment thinker John Locke, who is otherwise counted to liberal free thinking, in the area of the fight against poverty spoke for constraints on freedom, rigorous penal practice and command economy.

4 However, one should not overlook that Ronald Reagan, contrary to the monetarist credo of 'sound state finances' led an active policy of running up debts, which bloated the military budget (Star Wars Project etc.). In this respect, Reagan's policy remained 'Keynesian' (military Keynesianism).

5 Hitchens reports the case of 30-year-old single mother in Missouri, who was forced by the District Job Placement Scheme to work for a starvation-level wage at the food concern Tyson Foods. Her task was to pluck and draw chicken. While she was pregnant, she was refused social aid. She had to walk six miles to work on foot 11 days after her baby was born. This is the reality behind the well-sounding rhetoric of 'jobs, jobs, jobs'.

6 Compare in particular the proposals from the ranks of the German Greens and the CSU to punish childlessness with reductions in the computation of pension and old-age-care insurance.

7 The experiences of the inter-war period have actually shown already that capital-funded pension systems are in no way more stable than solidarity-based pension systems. Several times the state had to save these systems from insolvency. Precisely these experiences, for example, after the Second World War in West Germany gave the decisive push to introduce the tax- and contribution-based system after the war.

8 European Commission: Proposal for a Guideline of the European Parliament and the Council concerning Activities of Institutions of Business Old-Age Insurance, Brussels, October 11, 2000; COM (2000) 507 final.

9 This sound scepticism at least for Germany is also reaffirmed by an expert opinion by the Deutsches Institut für Wirtschaftsforschung (DIW) for the Federal German Ministry of the Economy of October 2001. It showed on the contrary that demographic change will only have a relatively minor effect on the cost developments in the health system. Decisive for the costs, moreover, is not age, but the proximity to death: in the last year before death 1/3 of the life-long costs of health care are incurred; for younger dying people they are even considerably higher than for older people. Prognoses about the costs of medical progress, according to this opinion, depend to such an extent on the chosen assumptions that no dependable statements can be made for the medium to longer term. The DIW further established that also medical-technical progress in Germany in the last 3 decades could be digested without any effect on the contribution rate.

Literature

Adamy, Wilhelm (1995): Der europäische Sozialstaat (The European social state), in: Schmidthenner, Horst, ed. *Der schlanke Staat* (Der schlanke Staat), Hamburg, p. 218 ff.

Beckmann, Martin/Bieling, Hans-Jürgen/Deppe, Frank, ed. (2003): Eurokapitalismus und globale politische Ordnung (Eurocapitalism and global political order), Hamburg.

BEPG (2003) : Empfehlung der Kommission für die Grundzüge der Wirtschaftspolitik der Mitgliedsstaaten und der Gemeinschaft (2003-2006) (Recommendation of the Commission fort he Basic Features of Economic Policy of the Member State and the Community, 2003-2006).

Bieling, Hans-Jürgen, ed. (1995): Arbeitslosigkeit und Wohlfahrtsstaat in Westeuropa. 9 Länder im Vergleich (Unemployment and Welfare State in Western Europe. 9 countries compared), FEG Study, No. 7, Marburg.

Christen, Christian/Michel, Tobias/Rätz, Werner (2003): *Sozialstaat* (Social state), Attac Basis Text 6, Hamburg.

Deppe, Frank/Weiner, Klaus-Peter (1991): *Binnenmarkt 92. Zur Entwicklung der Arbeitsbeziehungen in Europa* (Domestic market 92: About the development of the labour relations in Europe), Hamburg.

EMPL (2003): Beschluss des Rates über die Leitlinien für beschäftigungspolitische Maßnahmen der Mitgliedstaaten (2003-2006) (Resolution of the Council concerning employment political measures of the member states, 2003-2006), July 22.

Esping-Andersen, Gösta (1990): The Three Worlds of Welfare Capitalism, Princeton.

ETUC (1995): Die Aufwertung des europäischen Sozialmodells (The re-evaluation of the European social model), in: *Blätter für deutsche und internationale Politik* 8, p. 101 ff.

European Commission (1993): Weißbuch Wachstum, Wettbewerbsfähigkeit, Beschäftigung (White Book Economic Growth, Economic Competitiveness, Employment).

European Commission (1994): Weißbuch zur Sozialpolitik (White Book about Social Policy), p. 9.

European Commission (1997): Mitteilung zur Modernisierung des Sozialschutzes (Memorandum concerning the modernisation of the social state).

European Commission (1999): Eine konzertierte Strategie zur Modernisierung des Sozialschutzes (A concerted action concerning the modernisation of social protection).

European Commission (1999a): Long-term economic and budgetary implications of ageing populations, *European Economy*, No. 69.

European Commission (2000): Proposal for a directive on the activities of institutions for occupational retirement provision, October.

European Commission (2002): Mitteilung zur Straffung der wirtschafts- und beschäftigungspolitischen Koordinierung im Rahmen der Lisboner Strategie (Memorandum about the tightening of the economic and employment political coordination in the framework of the Lisbon strategy).

European Commission (2003): Mitteilung 'Stärkung der sozialen Dimension der Lisboner Strategie: Straffung der offenen Koordinierung im Bereich Sozialstaat' (Memorandum, Strengthening of the social dimension of the Lisbon strategy: Tightening of open coordination in the area of the social state).

European Commission (2003)/BEPG 2003: Empfehlung der Kommission für die Grundzüge der Wirtschaftspolitik der Mitgliedsstaaten und der Gemeinschaft (im Zeitraum 2003-2005); COM (2003) 170 (01) (Recommendation of the Commission concerning the Basic Tenets of the Economic Policy of the Member States and the Community; in the period 2003-2005).

European Council (2000): Schlussfolgerung des ER von Nizza (Conclusion of the European Council of Nice), December.

European Council (2003a): Joint Report on adequate and sustainable pensions.

European Council (2003b): Joint report by the Commission and the Council on supporting national strategies on the future of health care and care for the elderly.

European Policy Committee (2000): Progress report to the Ecofin Council on the impact of ageing populations on public pension systems, November.

Economic Policy Committee (2002): Reform challenges facing public pension systems: the impact of certain parametric reforms on pension expenditure, July.

Guibentif, P./Bouget, D. (1997): Les politiques du revenue minimum dans l'union Européenne (The politics of minimal revenue in the European Union), Lisbon.

Hertensteiner Programm der Europa-Union Deutschlands (Hertenstein Programme of the Europaunion of Germany) (http://www.europa-web.de/europa/02wwswww/205herte/hertenst.htm).

Hitchens, Christopher (1999): *No one left to lie to. The triangulations of William Jefferson Clinton*, London- New York.

Keynes, J.M. (1943): Das Langzeitproblem der Vollbeschäftigung (The long-term problem of full employment), in: Reuter, Norbert (1998): *Wachstumseuphorie und Verteilungsrealität* (Growth euphoria and the reality of distribution), Marburg, p. 139 ff.

Killdal, Nanna (2000): Workfare tendencies in Scandinavian welfare policies, manuscript.

Leibfried, Stefan/Pierson, Paul, ed. (1995): European Social Policy – Between

Fragmentation and Integration, Washington, D.C.
Manifesto of Ventotene (http://www.federaleurope.org/de/archives/ventotene.html).
Mühlbach, Paul (1950): Soziales Europa (Social Europe), in *Gewerkschaftliche Monatshefte* 5/1950.
Piven, Frances Fox (1998): Welfare and Work, in: *Social Justice* 1/98.
Platt, Tony (2004): Wieder eine Sache von Zucht und Mildtätigkeit. Geschichte und Gegenwart der Wohlfahrt in den USA (Again a matter of discipline and charity. History and present of welfare in the USA), in: *Sozialismus*, 1-2004.
Rheinländer, Martin (1999): Auf dem 3. Weg ins 21. Jahrhundert? (On the third road into the 21st century?), Manuscript.
Urban, Hans-Jürgen (2003): Die Neue Sozialpolitik. Zum Zusammenhang von europäischer Integration und nationalstaatlichem Sozialabbau (The new social policy: About the relationship between European integration and social demolition at the level of the national state), in: *Z* No. 55, September.
Von Oertzen, Peter (1984): Für einen neuen Reformismus (For a new reformism), Hamburg.

Chapter Four

The Future of the Social State in Europe

Eight Theses

André Brie MEP

The Keynesian welfare state, as we have seen, has been under constant fire since the end of the 1970s. Up until the 1990s, the prevailing pattern was to shrink the social safety net within the established system by cuts in unemployment benefit, pensions, the health service, and the like. Since the mid-1990s, the policy of cuts has been combined with a 'systemic reordering': the partial privatisation of pension systems; the primacy of personal self-provision; restructuring labour market policy in accordance with the philosophy of workfare; the creation of competitively organised educational, post-graduate training, and health markets. It seems that the Keynesian welfare state, in this way, will disappear sooner or later, and yield its place to a competition-oriented market.

The political left in Europe vacillates mainly between the option of an 'adaptation of the social state to the conditions of globalisation' and the 'defence of the achieved'. It tends to be minorities who want to put the social state on a new foundation – in Germany, the pertinent keywords are 'value creation tax', 'citizen and gainfully employed insurance', 'social basic insurance', and so on.[1] Broad, defensive mass protests by trade unions and social movements in Europe including general strikes (Greece 2001, Italy 1994/95, 2002/03, Spain and Portugal 2002, Austria and France 2003, Germany 2003 and 2004) have been able, at times, to delay the continuous social demolition and the liberalisation and privatisation of public property and services in the member states of the European Union, but not to stop it. From defence and protest to an alternative is, apparently, a long and arduous endeavour. Nevertheless, we cannot avoid asking ourselves the question: what has to be changed in order to maintain and renew the social state?

Thesis 1

The 'social state class compromise' has only modified the basic asymmetrical distribution of power between capital and labour, it has not structurally dissolved it. The compromise functioned under the good weather conditions of the long post-war upswing, until the beginning of the 1970s, but only as long as high growth rates offered the basis for distributing the increases in output. Thus, in a somewhat abbreviated manner, ran the core of the thesis of *social state illusion*. According to this argument, a fundamental systemic transformation to a socialist society is the only way that holds the long-term promise of overcoming this power asymmetry, and the harmful social consequences linked to it. A mere concentration on 'just compensation' and the transformation of secondary distribution by way of social state instruments promises no permanently stable solution in the interest of the great majority of the population dependent on gainful employment.

This position can call upon Karl Marx: 'If the material conditions of production are the cooperative property of the workers themselves, there also results a distribution of means of consumption different from the one prevailing today. Vulgar socialism (and in turn as part of democracy) took over from the bourgeois economists the observation and treatment of distribution as independent of the mode of production and the presentation of socialism, as if it turned mainly around the question of distribution.' (Marx: *Critique of the Gotha Programme*).[2]

If, together with Marx, we ask ourselves a question about the 'socialist way of production' which, among other things, would rely on a democratic socialisation of the means of production, and would include the moment when we 'produce differently, live differently' – what concretely would we have to imagine? As we know, Marx and Engels shirked this question, because it contradicted their idea of 'scientific socialism'. Instead, they criticised the 'sectarians' and 'Utopians' who imagined another society concretely as unscientific dreamers and handicraft modellers, far removed from reality. Only a field of ruins remains of the 'real socialism' of the Soviet period. Economically, it was not fit for survival; nor was it especially emancipating in socio-political terms. The assumption that a liberated society would result immediately from overcoming capitalist property relations in a certain way (state ownership of the means of production) has proved to be too simplistic. For the rest, there is at this point no developed debate about alternative visions of a socialist society, not even about the old social-democratic demand for 'economic democracy'. What follows practically, therefore, from the call for a 'socialist alternative', which springs from the thesis of 'social state illusion'?

To start with, there is not even a well anchored 'construction site' of theory. The anti-globalisation movement is only just starting to think about concepts such as global public goods, new property forms in the 'knowledge society' (free software, 'copyleft'), about participative budgets, and the strengthening of communal democracy ('reclaiming the state'). Usually it does this in a framework which is quite clearly oriented towards 'reform' in the Keynesian sense. Small circles of leftist intellectuals belabour questions of 'market socialism' or 'participative planning' at a high level of abstraction. One can learn quite a few things from such sources, but the debate is at best just starting. It is still far from offering more concrete projects for political and economic strategies, whether in the sense of 'market socialism' or a 'participative economy' (parecon). To develop these approaches further and make them fit for 'daily life' will probably take a long time, and require public and political resonance. This would be part of a serious debate about the future of the social state and conceptions of a 'socialist social state'.[3]

But let us not think that the social state is now a 'mere illusion'. Even in Britain, after the deep cuts of the neo-liberal revolution under Margaret Thatcher, social provision still accounts for about 27% of gross domestic product, which is close to the European Union average. It cannot be killed off as quickly as many right-wing ideologues would wish. Apparently, once a particular course of social development has been taken, it cannot easily be erased. Without the instruments of the Keynesian welfare state, now in the process of being demolished, the social reality and the crisis in Europe would look much more brutal than they currently do. Even though only the secondary distribution has been touched by it, it is an achievement to be defended, and a point of departure for more.

Thesis 2

In 1952, Gerhard Mackenroth, the theoretician of the social state, formulated a fundamental insight: 'that all social expense must always be covered from the popular income of the *current period*.' Whether social protection, social insurance, universal social basic insurance, capital-covered or tax-based mechanism – the sentence holds for everything in equal measure: 'there is no accumulation of funds, no transfer of shares of income as a source of social expense... The problem of national economics cannot be solved or pushed aside by acting according to the principles of an ordinary businessman and insuring private risks. At the national economic level, there does not exist an accumulation of consumption funds which can be consumed when needed, and which can then, in a way, be a welcome addition to the popular income of a later period.'

The financial markets are in no way a miracle weapon for 'saving the social system', as many politicians and economists want us to believe. The system of capital coverage is dependent on a permanent rise in productivity and, for example, on financing consumption in old age by restraining the gainfully employed from immediate consumption (thus, on saving).

Individuals may put aside money for tomorrow by saving today. A national economy as a whole cannot do that. It can guarantee social consumption in the future only by real physical and social investment today. The return on a pension fund or life insurance has to be produced in the current period. If this is not possible, the expected increase in value is lost.

Nor does international trade with obligations (for example, pension funds) solve this basic problem. This is because the capital that flows in from abroad (through the purchase of 'German' or 'European' securities) has first to be produced, and is subtracted from the gross domestic product of these countries. This also holds the other way around – one should only think of the glorious idea that European pension funds should invest in Chinese stocks and bonds and the Chinese workers are then supposed to produce 'our pensions'. Whichever way one turns it, one economic truism always holds: *There is no such thing as a free lunch!*

Before it is simply claimed that 'we' can no longer afford the social state, two questions pose themselves:

1 How is the popular income currently *produced?* (Karl Marx's core question)

and

2 How is it *distributed* (the equally justified core question of the old social-democratic workers' movement), so that sufficient social expenditure in the current period can be served out of it?

The economy of Europe no longer grows as rapidly as it did in the 1950s and 1960s, but it is still growing. If we 'save' on social expenditures under these conditions, other social groups may receive a larger share of the national income.

Thesis 3

Many look at the controversy about the social state almost exclusively from the point of view of 'social justice'. This is surely important. At first, however, we have to remember '*It's the economy, stupid!*' In times of high mass unemployment, there is the need first to try to come to terms with the *political economy of the social state*.

Heiner Flassbeck has pronounced a truth at first bitter for the left: 'The conflict over justice, the social safety net and solidarity in society is completely meaningless in times of high and rising unemployment. In such times, any measure that creates 100,000 jobs is considered just; any renunciation of wages, social protection or insurance protection which brings others wages and bread, as solidarity-inspired to the highest degree.'

It is, after all, not an accident that in the last 25 years large parts of the trade unions also believed the general propaganda that every one had to 'tighten their belts' and save from the point of view of the trade unions 'in a socially just way', so that the entrepreneurs, the high income earners, and wealth holders were also just a little bit fleeced. The background to this is the static and continuously high mass unemployment, which apparently cannot be addressed. It can hardly come any better for the executioners of the social state: the general logic of austerity and an apparently necessary flexibility is widely accepted. The dispute is no longer about the economy, but about who, in the name of 'solidarity', has to make what contribution to the general 'saving'.

From the economic point of view, however, the following question has to be asked: when the state as well as private households both restrain their expenditures, in other words 'save', how then should the entrepreneurs (quite independently of who owns them) expand sales and be able again to invest more? If some entrepreneurs now try to improve their situation by constant 'cost reductions' (of wages, wage supplements, and so on), they will only worsen the position of other entrepreneurs and the demand potential of other households. In the round that then follows, the state has less tax income and higher expenditures, because there are more unemployed people. Nothing comes of the envisaged budgetary consolidation and the debt reduction – new holes have to be mended. This cycle is known as the 'debt paradox'. From the point of view of the whole economy, this policy, socially as well as economically, leads to a downward spiral in which, in the end, everybody loses. It is not only socially unjust but also wrong, precisely from the point of view of economic policy. Current popular income stays far below what it could be, and what could be achieved by way of *another economic and financial policy*.

Thesis 4

Keynes clearly pointed to the connections between the economy, distribution, the social state and developed strategies, and how they can be worked to achieve durable 'well-being for all'. In his conception, the social and welfare state was embedded in an expansive macroeconomic policy for full employment, state investment guidance, control of the financial markets, curbing of speculation and a more balanced distribution of income and wealth.

Against this argument, it is today held that such a policy would only have any chance at all under conditions of closed national economies, not under those of 'globalisation'. A series of emerging industrial economies have pursued a more strongly domestically-oriented strategy (for example, Thailand, Malaysia, China, and Argentina after the crash). They have at least shown that they are able to achieve better economic results than those applying the neo-liberal mantras of structural adjustment.[4] For Europe within the European Union, another argument is much more decisive: 'since less than 10% of the gross domestic product of the European Union is exported to non-

EU countries, it is no exaggeration to characterise the European Union as a closed economy.' (Kleinknecht/Wengel 1998, p. 641). The medium and small European national state may have become too small to deal with economic problems, but the European Union as a whole is not.

This also means that social, tax and environmental standards can be regulated at a European level, and thus be withdrawn from global competition. A co-ordinated European tax and financial policy for solid and distributively just financing of the social tasks of the member states, co-ordinated economic policy for strengthened public investments in social infrastructure and environmental structural change, co-ordinated monetary and budgetary policy for the strengthening of the European domestic economy, and the environmentally sound revival of domestic demand — all this can be worth it and lead to full employment.[5] The social state in Europe can thus be maintained and renewed.

Ecologists criticise Keynes' strategy as fixated upon growth. High economic growth increases environmental problems because of the greater consumption of energy and raw materials. This criticism of Keynes, however, is only partly justified: 'The Keynesian long-term strategy (Keynes, 1943), which prognosticated lessening growth (stagnation) for the highly developed national economies, such that it would no longer be possible to achieve full employment in the traditional way of high growth rates, did not usher in a elaborate new edition of growth stimulating politics, but Keynes did recommend already more than half a century ago in the middle of the Second World War (1943!) step-wise reductions in labour time. The argument for this way back to full employment is also supported by the most recent ecological problem discussion: ultimately, any kind of growth harms the economy, so that also in the future, it will be necessary to solve the employment and social problems also without (high) economic growth rates.' (Karl Georg Zinn 2003).

Zinn's proposal of a 'qualitative Keynesianism', at least as a transitional programme in the medium term (20 to 30 years), has some plausibility. In common with Marx and political ecology, it places changing 'the exchange of materials with nature' in the foreground: ecological and social restructuring for sustainable development. At the margins of the trade union and environmental movement, there has already developed a basic framework for a comprehensive, sustainable strategy. The recommended individual tools certainly require discussion, but the fundamental logic of alternative development points in the correct direction.

Ecological innovation on a broad front leads to a multitude of new products and services: solar-hydrogen-economy, fuel cells, drastic energy and resource saving, ecological farming, plant-based chemistry, bionics, ethno-botany, green information technology, mobility and energy services. It will take a while, until new satisfaction levels are reached in this way. Environmental innovation is closely linked with social innovation: eco-efficient services, the extension of social and cultural services, social citizenship rights, rights of economic democracy, education and qualification, a new working-time standard, and 'Useful Work'. The return to high growth rates is not at the centre: rather, a far-reaching dematerialisation of the economy, and the targeted improvement of the living conditions of the majority of the population.

Qualitative Keynesianism thus promotes lasting, ecologically sound and just well-being for all. It is fully compatible with far-reaching eco-socialist concepts. And it creates an economic environment in which a social state that has been renewed on the basis of solidarity can be embedded.

Thesis 5

Then there is the question of the 'demographic challenge'. On present trends, by the year 2050, the proportion of people in Europe who are aged over 65 will have doubled; after that the population will begin to shrink significantly. This is seen only as a cost problem. The demographic changes will be met by cuts in pensions and health systems, and the instruction to make 'more private provision'.

But the 'cost problem' of an ageing and shrinking population can be met comparatively easily. By maintaining the average growth in productivity of the past 100 years, Europe will be in a position to sustain welfare even with a shrinking proportion of the population gainfully employed, and so guarantee adequate material security for both young and old equally. There is no doubt that the tax and contribution basis for financing social security systems for the elderly has to be broadened, and income and wealth differentials have to be reduced more sharply.

The political mainstream, however, does not ask the really important questions: how do work and living conditions have to be changed so that people can stay healthy and happy in gainful employment, and can remain so when they reach retirement age? Which social, educational and other infrastructures are needed in a society where the proportion of elderly and older people continues to increase over several decades? And how should the life conditions of children and young people be designed, so that they can develop in an all-round way?

For the future, we must seek deceleration, sufficiency, distributive justice, health promotion and individual freedom, instead of more inequality, market constraint, ever more stress, and entrepreneurial 'flexibility'. The solution to the demographic question requires more social provision and a better social state, in parallel to the necessary changes in work and economic life.

Thesis 6

In light of the diversity of welfare state traditions in the European Union, the debate about a renewal of the social state in Europe can be maintained only at the level of guiding images and functions, which the social security systems are thus supposed to fulfil.

Socialist policy stands for a social state that guarantees social citizenship rights materially by way of universal and unconditional services in the framework of a public all-encompassing insurance.[6] Health, education, protection against social risks, and so on have to be considered as *public goods*, which should be withdrawn from market compulsion and market forces. From there, as a guiding vision for the renewal of the social security systems, there follows the concept of a people's or citizens' insurance. Contribution requirements (whether as taxes or social contributions) and claims for services tie in with *inhabitant status,* and no longer exclusively with gainful employment, as was the case in the conservative-corporatist welfare state.

The financing of the tasks of the social state is to be borne by all inhabitants (female and male) and businesses according to their financial capability. Thus, the basis of contribution will be broadened, and the principle of solidarity-based redistribution strengthened. There exists a considerable spectrum of proposals on how this general guiding image is to be implemented concretely. In the context of the German Federal Republic, some propose to finance social security generally by way of a value-creation tax. Thus, part of the value created would be taken out of the conflict over primary distribution (between capital and labour) and reserved exclusively to finance social-state tasks. Others envisage replacing the employers' contribution to social insurance by a value-creation tax. Still others want to extend the contribution base of the social security system (for example, to self-employed people, civil servants, housewives, and so on), as well as with respect to the inclusion of other kinds of income (for example, rent, interest and capital returns). In this context, reference is often made to already existing national state models of a 'citizen insurance' (for example, health insurance in Austria, pension insurance in Switzerland). The strengths and weaknesses as well as the consequences of the respective 'models' are tied predominantly to the national context, and should be evaluated in this framework. They all have in common that they imply a completely different direction for social state renewal than the 'social reforms' now being implemented in the member states, and the current socio-political guiding vision at the level of the European Union.

Socialist politics strives for comprehensive equality between women and men. At odds with this are the social concepts of normality, which are imbued with the patriarchal image of the male head of the household and which still characterise most social states in the European Union. The renewal of the social state has to overcome the multiple disadvantages of women and insist on egalitarian patterns of gainful employment: equal payment for work of equal value, equal career opportunities, shorter work times and access to protected part-time work for both sexes. Independent tax and social systems can be taken up on this basis; that is, the abolition of the social and tax policy privileges of the 'housewife marriage' and the 'marital partnership'. Whether people live together with or without a marriage certificate is their affair. The tax and social system should not favour one or the other arrangement.

Thus, the advantages enjoyed by the married couple have to be completely removed from family policy. There remains the simple sentence: family is where there are children. In this respect, the renewal of the social state has to be above all service-oriented: an area-wide extension of public child-care centres, which makes possible the compatibility of family and profession. A targeted financial support of households with children ('family burden compensation') is to be borne in solidarity by the whole community, in the form of tax-financed basic child allowances.

Socialist policy strives for basic social security, which prevents poverty and enables equal participation in social well-being (participative justice). Security in old age is to be achieved by solidarity-based, redistributive public systems. It must fulfil two functions: basic social security in old age (as basic security for all) and maintenance of adequate living standards (performance justice). Periods of child-rearing, caring for elderly relatives, and basic and post-graduate training, as well as phases of unemployment and sickness have to be adequately taken into account. The health system including long-term care has to be financed on the basis of solidarity (an income-proportional and thereby redistributive contribution assessment), and must provide qualitatively high-level services to all independent of their income. A 'citizen insurance system' in this context allows a more targeted prevention policy (and thereby opens considerable cost-reduction potentials) than a market-economy dismembered health system. Unemployment support has to remain an unconditional social legal claim, guarantee freedom of choice of occupation, and uphold and renew already acquired qualifications.

The repair of all three pillars of social protection — care for the elderly, health care, and gainful employment — requires a new policy of full employment and social redistribution (compare Thesis 4). Without this, an egalitarian renewal of the social state will not succeed.

Thesis 7

In the European Union, the social state is primarily developed at the level of the national state, and this in very different ways. In accordance with the dogma of strengthening 'competitiveness', a harsh regime of competition between the national social states has been established. The member states are constantly tempted to achieve a competitive edge by demolishing social benefits. Thus, the question at the European level is, first of all, to prevent increased social dumping in the extended European Union.

Agreement on a social stability pact is necessary to achieve this goal. This builds on the simple fact that there exists a very close connection between the economic development of a country (measured as gross domestic product per head), and its social performance quota (the share of all social expenditure in gross domestic product).

In the framework of a social stability pact, the social performance quotas of the 25 European Union member states would first be recorded and countries with similar quotas put together in a group ('corridor'). A downward departure from the initial value would entail a consultation procedure for the countries concerned and, if necessary, sanctions. In this way, social development would be coupled to economic development. The more weakly developed national economies in the European Union would not be over-taxed by this form of social policy regulation. The more they gained in economic development, the more their social performance quotas would approach those in the rest of the European Union. The economically stronger member countries would thus have their way barred to social dumping (under average social benefit quotas in relation to their income level).

The European Union can and must do considerably more than just prevent social dumping. In the future it must set binding, quantitative and qualitative social policy tasks: for example, for the improvement of health insurance, for the minimal level of social protection, for European minimum wage standards, for overcoming poverty, social exclusion, homelessness and illiteracy. It has to be possible, within this framework, to commit the member states to concrete programmes whose implementation will be continually analysed and controlled. The European Union can supplement these programmes by European promotion. Thus, European social policy would begin to have an independent effect, beyond merely gathering information, agreeing indicators and comparing 'best practices'.

In the perspective of social policy, there is also the question of the 'finality of European integration' – towards which goal should it ultimately strive? Within the framework of a federal or confederated European Union, don't we also need a European social union ('Social State European Union'), as was demanded by the anti-fascist movements in Europe after the Second World War? Is it sensible to lay down, at the European level, unified norms for standards of service, levels of benefits, and additional entitlements, as well as adaptations of rules?[7] Core ingredients of social security, for example, might be basic social security, old age and invalidity pensions, unemployment support, family benefits, and health services. In this way, the manifold practical problems that have until now beset the 'coordination of social protection systems' in the areas of free mobility and freedom of residence of persons, would resolve themselves.

The key to such a solution lies in choosing relative reference parameters: for example, as far as a European basic social security is concerned, there should be a benefit level of 60% of the national average income of the member state, in which a person chooses to reside. Thus, there would be no incentive to 'social tourism' – for example, by taking along the relatively generous basic social protection provided in the Netherlands when settling in regions with low living costs such as Apulia or Extremadura if, for instance, the national state social insurance were to be made 'transportable' all over Europe. The economic performance of the respective member state of residence would be duly taken into account by the choice of relative reference parameters.

Today, this debate still sounds like the distant music of the future. But if one wants to prevent the increased 'Europe-wide patient mobility' that is presently being discussed and opens the way to a European Union domestic market in health services, which would gradually undermine the solidarity-based health systems of the national states that have already been severely hit by the recent 'health reforms', then one also has to think about European solutions.

Thesis 8

What are the social and political forces that can produce a dynamic in the direction of a social Europe?

Under present conditions, these are still relative minorities: they are the trade unions, acting up now mainly at the level of the nation state, which are opposed to social demolition; the social movements coming together in the European Social Forum (ESF), voluntary organisations and initiatives: and the European left-wing parties as well as minority tendencies in the European Greens and Social Democrats.

The European Social Forum undoubtedly makes an important contribution to creating a European democratic political public – alongside the formations of European political parties and foundations as well as existing European associations and networks. With the European days of action by the European Trade Union Confederation (ETUC) and the social movements on April 2 and 3, 2004, perhaps a beginning was made to going beyond resistance to social state demolition at the national state level to a discussion about a common European perspective and capability for action.

In this respect, nobody should be taken in by the illusion that it might be possible to compensate, at a European level, for defeats at the local, regional or national levels. The fight for a social Europe must rather be viewed as an initiative within a political system of several levels. In this respect, the social state, public services, and existing public provision can be defended at the local, regional and national levels. But if it is not possible to back up this policy with a European dimension (the social stability pact, Social Union), these efforts are always structurally on the defensive. The European Union's economic policy, its growth and stability pact, and its policy of deregulation in the domestic market all continuously erode progress. Without the perspective of a turn in this developmental logic also at the European level, these struggles remain precarious and incomplete.

If we succeed in building up a European dimension of resistance against the demolition of the social state, this in turn can have positive feedback for the activities in the same direction at the national, regional and local levels. After all, nothing is more inspiring than to discover common concerns with a multitude of sympathetic minds and to see one's own activities reinforced and supported by those of others. In the present phase, the issue will mainly be whether, by common European discussion and activities, a minimum consensus can emerge between the participants concerning core elements in the renewal of the social state, which then develops persuasive influence on social majorities. When the widespread belief that 'there is no alternative' is for the first time seriously challenged, then it will become possible to gradually overcome the present defensive situation.

Translated by Carla Krüger

Notes

1 Concerning the concept of financing of the social insurances by way of a value creation tax in Germany compare Christen/Kahrs/Weise 2000. The concepts of the German green and alternative Left from the 1980s and 1990s concerning the 'citizens and gainfully employed insurance' and the 'social basic insurance' have meanwhile, by the Agenda 2010 and the Rürup Commission, received a radical reinterpretation. Compare on that critically Bartelheimer 2003 and Kreutz 2003.

2 Marx by the way even declined to speak about a 'social question', which lies at the basis of the later discourse about the social state: 'In the stead of the existing class struggle, there enters a newspaper writer phrase – the 'social question', whose 'solution' one 'prepares the ground for'. Instead of from the revolutionary transformation process of society the 'socialist organisation of total labour' 'emerges' from the 'state help' that the state gives to productive cooperatives, which *it*, not the worker, 'calls into being'. This is worthy of the imagination of Lassalle that one can with state obligations build a new society just as well as a new railroad!' (Marx: *Critique of the Gotha Programme*)

3 Marx has addressed the latter question in the criticism of the Gotha Programme. He referred to the fact that from the 'products of labour' there also had to be formed 'funds for those incapable of working', for 'common needs' such as schools and health institutions as well as 'insurance against accidents and disturbances'.

4 My reference pertains not only to the quantitative economic results (increase in the GDP and the national popular income), with which the mainstream economists are after all mainly concerned in their argumentation. That the social position of people, the income distribution, the income pollution etc. in these countries are anything else but desirable, stands on another leaf, and this can also only be changed by different social relationships of forces and corresponding political conceptions in these countries themselves.

5 More concrete proposals for such policies I have submitted some time ago (compare Brie/Dräger 2001, Brie 2002). Much of it can also be found in the programme of the PDS for the European elections.

6 The same is also claimed by the Scandinavian social-democratic welfare state model; yet, social democracy in Sweden has also introduced its reconstruction. However, it should still be stressed that the Scandinavian model in the EU comparison economically as well as socially still achieves better results than the others (comp. Corsi/Orsini 2001).

7 Compare the discussion of different solutions for example in Leibfried 1992 und Busch 1998.

Literature

Albert, Michael (2003): *PARECON – Life after Capitalism*, London.

Balakrishnan, Gopal (2003): Algorithms of War, in: *New Left Review* 23, September/October.

Bartelheimer, Peter (2003): An der richtigen Stelle Nein sagen. Von der bündnisgrünen Idee einer sozialen Grundsicherung bleibt in der Agenda 2010 nichts mehr übrig (The art to say No at the right point. Of the Green/Bündnis 90 Idea of a Social Basic Insurance, there remains nothing in the Agenda 2010), in *Frankfurter Rundschau*, June 12, 2003.

Bischoff, Joachim/Menard, Michael (1990): *Marktwirtschaft und Sozialismus* (Market economy and socialism), Hamburg.

Bobbit, Phillip (2002): *The shield of Achilles. War, Peace and the Course of History*, New York.

Brie, André/Dräger, Klaus (2000): New Europe – New Economy? Alternatives for a social and ecological Europe, www.pds-europa.de.

Brie, André (2002): Eine alternative Agenda für Vollbeschäftigung (An alternative agenda for full employment), www.pds-europa.de.

Busch, Klaus (1998): Das Korridormodell: ein Konzept zur Weiterentwicklung der EU-Sozialpolitik (The corridor model: a concept for the further development of the EU social policy), in: *Politik und Gesellschaft Online/International Politics and Society* 2/1998.

Corsi, Marcella/Orsini, Kristian (2001): Poverty rates in Europe, manuscript

Creydt, Meinhard (2001): Partizipatorische Planung und Sozialisierung des Marktes (Participative planning and socialisation of the market), in *Widerspruch* 40, Zürich.

Christen, Christian/Kahrs, Horst/Weise, Klaus (2000): Wertschöpfungsabgabe statt lohnbezogener Arbeitgeberanteile zu den gesetzlichen Sozialversicherungen (Value-creation tax instead of wage-based employers' contributions to the legal social insurances), Berlin (http.//archiv14.pds-im-bundestag.de/themen/arso/wertschoepfungsabgabe/wertschoepfungsstudie.pdf).

Eichenhofer, Eberhard (2003): Reform des Sozialstaats – von der Arbeitnehmerversicherung zur Einwohnersicherung? (Reform of the Social State – from the Employee protection to the inhabitant insurance?) in: *Recht der Arbeit* 5, p. 264-269.

Elson, Diane (1990): Markt-Sozialismus oder Sozialisierung des Marktes (Market Socialism or Socialisation of the Market), in: *Prokla H. 78*, Berlin.
Flassbeck, Heiner (2003): Wie Deutschland wirtschaftlich ruiniert wurde, Ein Bericht aus dem Jahr 2010 (How Germany was ruined economically, A Report from the year 2010), in: *Blätter für deutsche und internationale Politik* 8/2003, pp. 955-965.
Hans-Böckler-Stiftung, ed. (2000): Arbeit und Ökologie (Work and Ecology), Berlin/Wuppertal.
Kleinknecht, Alfred/ter Wengel, Jan (1998): The myth of economic globalisation, in: *Cambridge Journal of Economics*, vol. 22, no. 5, September.
Kickbusch, Ilona (2000): Das Soziale ist die beste Medizin (The social is the best medicine), Presentation at the Congress 'Poverty and Health', Berlin, manuscript.
Krätke, Michael (2002): Demokratisierung der Wirtschaft – Sozialisierung der Märkte (Democratisation of the economy – socialisation of the markets), in: *Widerspruch* 43.
Kreutz, Daniel (2003): Bürgerversicherung – Chance oder Risiko? (Citizens' insurance – chance or risk?), manuscript.
Liebfried, Stephan (1992): Europäische Integration zwischen Marktbürger und Marktfreiheit. Über die Chancen und Risiken eines Wohlfahrtsstaats (European Integration between market citizenship and market freedom. About the chances and risks of a welfare state), in: *Frankfurter Rundschau* of August 3, 1992 (Part 1) and August 8, 1992 (Part 2).
Mackenroth, Gerhard (1952): Die Reform der Sozialpolitik durch einen deutschen Sozialplan (The reform of social policy by way of a German social plan), in: Albrecht, G., ed.: *Schriften des Vereins für Sozialpolitik*, new edition, vol. 4, Berlin, p. 39-59.
PDS Europawahlprogramm (2004): Alternativen sind machbar: Für ein soziales, demokratisches und friedliches Europa! (Alternatives are feasible: for a social, democratic and peaceful Europe!), http://www.pds-online.de/wahlen/dokumnete/europawahlprogramm2004/index.htm.
Roemer, John (1994): *A Future for Socialism?*, London.
Roemer, John, ed. (1996): *Equal Shares*, London.
Spangenberg, Joachim, ed. (2003): Vision 2020. Arbeit, Umwelt, Gerechtigkeit – Strategien für ein zukunftsfähiges Deutschland (Vision 2020. Work, Environment, Justice – Strategies for a Germany capable of a future), Munich.
Zinn, Karl Georg (2003): *Die Zukunft eines qualitativen Keynesianismus in Europa* (The future of a qualitative Keynesianism in Europe), manuscript.

Chapter Five

Unemployment in Britain: What Are the Real Numbers?

Christina Beatty and Stephen Fothergill

Christina Beatty and Stephen Fothergill work at the Centre for Regional Economic and Social Research, Sheffield Hallam University.

Abstract

More than 2.5 million non-employed adults of working age in Britain claim sickness-related benefits, and the numbers have risen steeply over time. The very large variation in the numbers across districts and regions points strongly to extensive hidden unemployment, especially in older industrial areas affected by job losses. This article builds on two previous articles in *Regional Studies* – one dealing with the theoretical framework and the other a local case study – to present wholly new estimates of the scale of the diversion across all parts of the country. It also questions contemporary perceptions of the UK labour market and the validity of current approaches to re-engaging sickness claimants with employment.

Introduction

There is a widely held view among politicians and journalists that the United Kingdom's unemployment problem is all but solved. The UK labour market is increasingly seen as being characterised mainly by labour shortages, and residual unemployment is frequently attributed to failings in individual skills and motivation.

There is little doubt that the UK labour market has indeed improved substantially since the depths of the early 1990s recession, and that parts of southern England are now at or near full employment. However, the assertion that unemployment has all but faded away is based on serious misunderstandings about what has actually happened in the labour market. In particular, the denial of continuing and large-scale joblessness relies all too often on data that measures only part of the overall problem.

This paper explores what is probably the largest single distortion to the data – the diversion from unemployment to sickness benefits. In particular, the paper presents new and up-to-date estimates of the scale of the diversion and, for the first time, provides estimates of the size of the diversion in every region and district of Great Britain.

The first part of the paper explains how the UK benefits system works and how this gives rise to a diversion from recorded unemployment to recorded sickness. This is followed by a review of the existing evidence. The main body of the paper then presents estimates of the scale of the diversion, deploying a new and improved method that provides more robust estimates at the local and regional scale. The final part comments on the nature of this form of unemployment, on the implications for perceptions of the contemporary UK labour market, and on the policies likely to move the British economy closer to genuine full employment.

Two benefit systems

It is not widely recognised that in the UK two separate benefit systems provide support to non-employed adults of working age.

The first relates to 'unemployment'. Since 1996 this has taken the form of Jobseeker's Allowance (JSA). To claim JSA a person must demonstrate that they are available for work and looking for work, and they must 'sign on' once every two weeks. For most claimants, including all those claiming for more than six months, JSA is means-tested (on the basis of household income).

The other benefit system relates to 'sickness'. Since 1995 this has taken the form of Incapacity Benefit (IB). IB is paid to non-employed adults of working age who have health problems or disabilities. About two-thirds of IB claimants actually receive Incapacity Benefit. The remaining third, with insufficient National Insurance (NI) credits to qualify for IB itself, are counted as 'NI credits only' claimants and in most cases actually receive means-tested Income Support with a disability premium. Importantly, Incapacity Benefit is not means-tested except for a small number of new claimants with substantial pension income. Also, although Incapacity Benefit payments start at almost the same rate as JSA they increase after six months and again after twelve months. The disability premium payable to 'NI credits only' IB claimants also makes this worth more than JSA.

The workings of the benefits system may seem a long way removed from the measurement of unemployment. The point is however that for many of the longer-term jobless who have health problems, the differential in benefit payments creates an incentive to claim IB rather than JSA. For example, an unemployed man with a wife in work and perhaps a small pension from a previous employer will not generally be entitled to means-tested JSA. In essence, his wife's earnings and his pension reduce or eliminate his JSA entitlement. But if he has sufficient health problems, and if he has enough NI credits (which most men with a work history do have), he will be eligible to claim Incapacity Benefit irrespective of his wife's earnings or in most circumstances of his pension as well.

The gatekeepers determining access to Incapacity Benefit are medical practitioners – initially the claimant's own GP but for claims beyond six months doctors working on behalf of the Benefits Agency. To qualify for IB a person must be deemed not fit enough to work. In practice, however, the tests applied by the Benefits Agency assess ability to undertake certain basic physical tasks rather than inability to do all kinds of work in all circumstances. Many unemployed people have picked up injuries over the course of their working life, and there is the effect on health and physical abilities of simply getting older. In practice, therefore, many of the unemployed with health problems are able to claim IB rather than JSA. As IB claimants they are not required to sign-on fortnightly or to look for work. Instead they will typically be recalled for medical re-assessment only once every two or three years.

The diversion onto Incapacity Benefit distorts both official measures of UK unemployment. The best known of these measures is the *claimant count* – the number of people out of work and claiming unemployment related benefits, mainly JSA but also NI credits for unemployment. In the UK benefits system, the men and women claiming unemployment-related benefits and those claiming sickness-related benefits are two mutually exclusive groups. None of the Incapacity Benefit claimants are therefore included in the claimant count.

The other measure of unemployment (and officially the preferred one, even though it is less often quoted) is the *ILO measure* derived from the Labour Force Survey. This uses the International Labour Organisation definition of unemployment which counts anyone who is out of work and wants a job, is available to start in the next two weeks, and has looked for work in the last four weeks. The ILO definition produces unemployment figures for Britain as a whole that in the last three or four years have been around half a million higher than the claimant count. In theory the ILO measure of unemployment is independent of benefit rules. In practice, because there is no requirement for IB claimants to look for work and because many think that they would not find suitable work, most IB claimants do not look for work. They therefore fail one of the ILO unemployment tests and drop out of the ILO unemployment figures as well as the claimant count.

The numbers claiming Incapacity Benefit are now truly astonishing. Figure 1 shows the number of men and women of working age (16-64 for men, 16-59 for women) claiming IB (or its predecessor Invalidity Benefit) for more than six months. The numbers have risen more or less continuously for two decades. In 1981 there were 570,000 men and women in this category. By 2003 the figure had risen to 2,130,000. Even this is not the full picture. Added to this there were more than 300,000 further claimants of working age receiving Severe Disablement Allowance (SDA), which is paid to people with a high degree of disability but insufficient NI credits to qualify for IB. There were also more than 200,000 short-term (ie. less than six months) IB claimants of working age. Official statistics show that in Britain as a whole in August 2003 a grand total of almost 2.7 million non-employed people of working age were claiming sickness-related benefits. Of these, 1.6 million were men and 1.1 million were women.

The big increase in the number of working-age men claiming sickness-related benefits was primarily a phenomenon of the 1980s and early 1990s. Thereafter, the number of long-term male claimants shown in Figure 1 tended to plateau with only a very small continuing increase. 1995 is a significant date in this regard in that it marks the changeover from Invalidity Benefit to Incapacity Benefit, which

Figure 1: Claimants of working age incapacitated by long-term* sickness and invalidity, 1981-2003, Great Britain

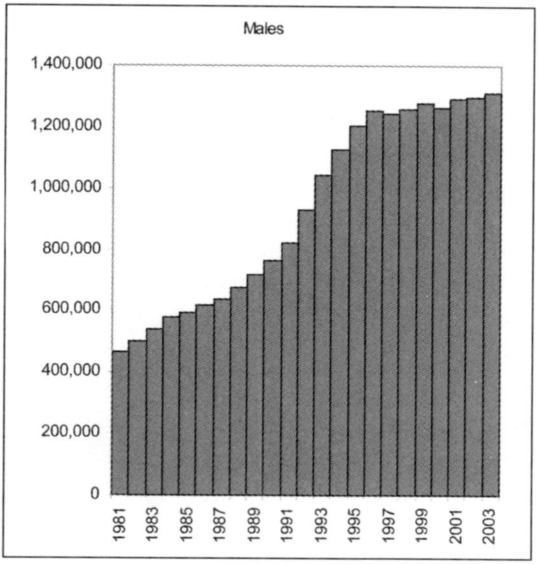

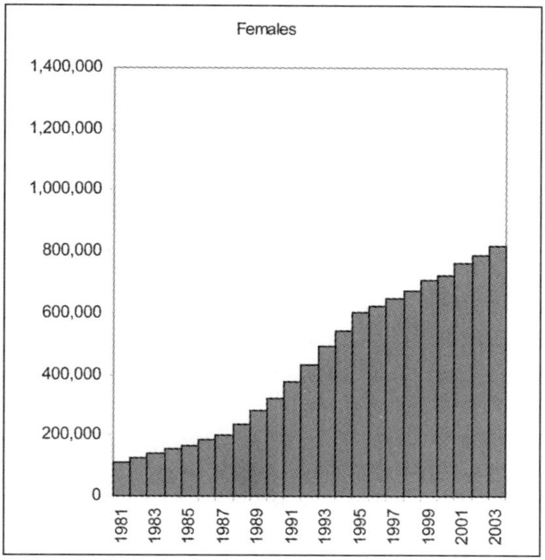

*for six months or more

Source: Social Security Statistics, Department of Work and Pensions

transferred responsibility for authorising longer-term claims from family doctors to doctors working on behalf of the Benefits Agency and introduced standardised assessment procedures. The number of women who are long-term IB claimants has in contrast shown an almost continuous increase, though the absolute level remains lower than for men. What the trends in Figure 1 also demonstrate is that the long period of economic growth in the British economy from around 1993 onwards made absolutely no dent in the number of long-term IB claimants.

It is highly unlikely that there has been a four-fold increase in the level of long-term incapacitating illness in the UK workforce over the last twenty years. Indeed, the increase has happened at a time when general standards of health are known to be showing a slow but steady improvement, admittedly with the slowest improvement among the most disadvantaged groups. Almost certainly, what can be observed in the rise in the number of long-term sickness claimants is to a great extent the interaction of a difficult labour market and the UK social security system.

Existing evidence

That the claimant count measure of UK unemployment is flawed is no longer disputed. Whilst it is accurate in counting those who are out of work and in receipt of unemployment-related benefits, what is accepted is that the claimant count is influenced by changes in benefit rules. There have been more than thirty of these since the early 1980s, not least the changeover from Unemployment Benefit to Jobseeker's Allowance, the effect of which was to cut the claimant count by reducing the duration for which non-means tested benefits were available and increasing the requirement to demonstrate active job-seeking. The criticisms of the claimant count have come from academic sources (for example Gregg 1994, MacKay 1999), from independent watchdogs such as the Unemployment Unit (Convery 1996) and from no less a source than the Royal Statistical Society (1995).

A study of the labour market in the UK coalfields in the wake of pit closures was one of the first to argue that there is a diversion from unemployment to sickness benefits (Beatty and Fothergill 1996). The study found that the largest single adjustment to job loss was a withdrawal of men into 'economic inactivity', and that the largest component of this withdrawal was a big increase in recorded 'permanent sickness'. In contrast, pit closures had virtually no impact at all on recorded unemployment in the coalfields. Subsequent similar studies of England's disadvantaged rural areas (Beatty and Fothergill 1997) and of seaside towns (Beatty and Fothergill 2003) also identified withdrawals from the labour market into 'sickness' as the key factor holding down recorded unemployment among men, though not on quite the same scale as in the coalfields. A study of Britain's cities (Turok and Edge 1999) likewise found that labour market withdrawal by men was a key response to job loss in the 1980s and early 1990s.

More generally, there is accumulating evidence that the disparities in employment opportunities between different parts of Britain are reflected less in unemployment data than in levels of economic inactivity among the working age population. Studies by Gregg and Wadsworth (1998), Green (1997,1999) and Green and Owen (1998) confirm this point. Mackay (1999) makes the observation that 'the greater the degree of labour market disadvantage, the less appropriate is unemployment as a measure of labour market slack'. The relevant point here is that whereas the unemployed (either claimant or ILO) are conventionally included among the economically active, claimants of sickness-related benefits such as Incapacity Benefit are nearly all included among the inactive.

The relationship between unemployment, ill health and the number claiming sickness-related benefits is nevertheless complex. In parallel with the argument that there has been a diversion from 'unemployment' to 'sickness' within the benefits system, there is a quite separate argument that unemployment is actually a cause of ill health. That there is a causal link from unemployment and poverty to ill health is in fact not disputed (see for example Bellaby and Bellaby 1999). Nor is the fact that the groups most at risk of unemployment are also the ones most likely to be affected by ill health (Bartley and Owen 1996). But these processes alone seem unable to account for the sheer number of sickness claimants in the UK, or the scale of the increase through time. The UK's General Household Survey, for example, records an increase of nearly a quarter in self-reported limiting long-term illness among men between the early 1980s and the late 1990s, but this increase is of a magnitude that seems unable to explain the huge increase in the number of sickness claimants. Moreover, General Household Survey data may reflect a greater willingness over time to report illnesses as much as any deterioration in underlying standards of health.

Beatty, Fothergill and Macmillan (2000) tried to reconcile the rising numbers claiming Incapacity Benefit with the observation that standards of health have not deteriorated to the same extent. They also tried to reconcile the rising numbers with the requirement for all IB claimants to demonstrate a significant degree of ill heath. The argument put forward was that work-limiting ill health is actually quite widespread in the working age population but that many of the men and women with health problems do in fact hold down jobs. This is confirmed by data from the Labour Force Survey (*Labour Market Trends* 2002) showing that of the estimated 7.2 million men and women of working age in the UK who had a work-limiting long-term illness or disability in winter 2001/02, 3.4 million were in employment.

Beatty, Fothergill and Macmillan argued that difficult labour market conditions such as those experienced in the UK for most of the 1980s and 90s expose men and women with health problems to job loss, and that when they find themselves out of work their health often places them at the back of the queue for jobs. These people have sufficient ill health to access sickness-related benefits instead of unemployment benefits – in other words their benefit claims are not fraudulent. The net effect, however, is that in a difficult labour market the ill heath that was once hidden because people were in work becomes visible in the numbers claiming sickness-related benefits. Furthermore, as the economy picks up it is the healthy job-seekers on unemployment benefits who are the first to be taken on again, leaving a large marginalized group on sickness benefits – precisely the experience in the UK labour market in the late 1990s and early 2000s.

The survey evidence on Incapacity Benefit claimants tends to confirm this perspective. Easterlow and Smith (2003) found that people experiencing ill health do not lack the incentive to work and are likely to be forced rather than lured onto pensions and onto benefits. Extensive survey work reported in Alcock et al (2003) confirms that although a degree of self-reported work-limiting ill health is just about universal among men claiming Incapacity Benefit, only a quarter say they can't do any work at all. The same survey evidence also shows that active job-seeking tails off badly among male Incapacity Benefit claimants, with barely one in twenty looking for work despite the fact that around half say they would like a full-time job and more than a quarter looked for work after their last job ended.

A survey of male Incapacity Benefit claimants in Barrow-in-Furness (Beatty and Fothergill 2002a), an area affected by major job losses in the local shipbuilding industry, provides further evidence that a substantial proportion of IB claimants should be regarded as hidden unemployed. In Barrow the age, skills and low qualifications of male IB claimants would anyway have exposed them to unemployment. Ill health was the reason for job loss in fewer than half of all cases, with redundancy often figuring strongly. Two-thirds of Barrow's male IB claimants said they would like a full-time job, and only a third said they could do no work at all.

Analyses of local and sectoral data offer additional evidence. Armstrong (1999) concluded that there is evidence of hidden male unemployment among sickness claimants in Northern Ireland. In North West England, Sutherland (1999) highlighted off-flows from claimant unemployment onto Incapacity Benefit. Fieldhouse and Hollywood (1999) found a strong movement of ex-miners into permanent sickness rather than recorded unemployment.

The geography of sickness benefit claimants

What is particularly striking is the distribution of sickness claimants across Britain. Figures 2 and 3 illustrate this point. They show the share of the total working age population, by district in August 2003, claiming sickness-related benefits – in this instance Incapacity Benefit (long and short-term and NI credits only) and Severe Disablement Allowance. The headline GB total at that time was 2,662,000, representing 7.5 per cent of the entire working age population. The data on the number of claimants in each district comes from the Department for Work and Pensions and is based on a 5 per cent

Figure 2: Adults of working age claiming sickness-related benefits, England and Wales, August 2003

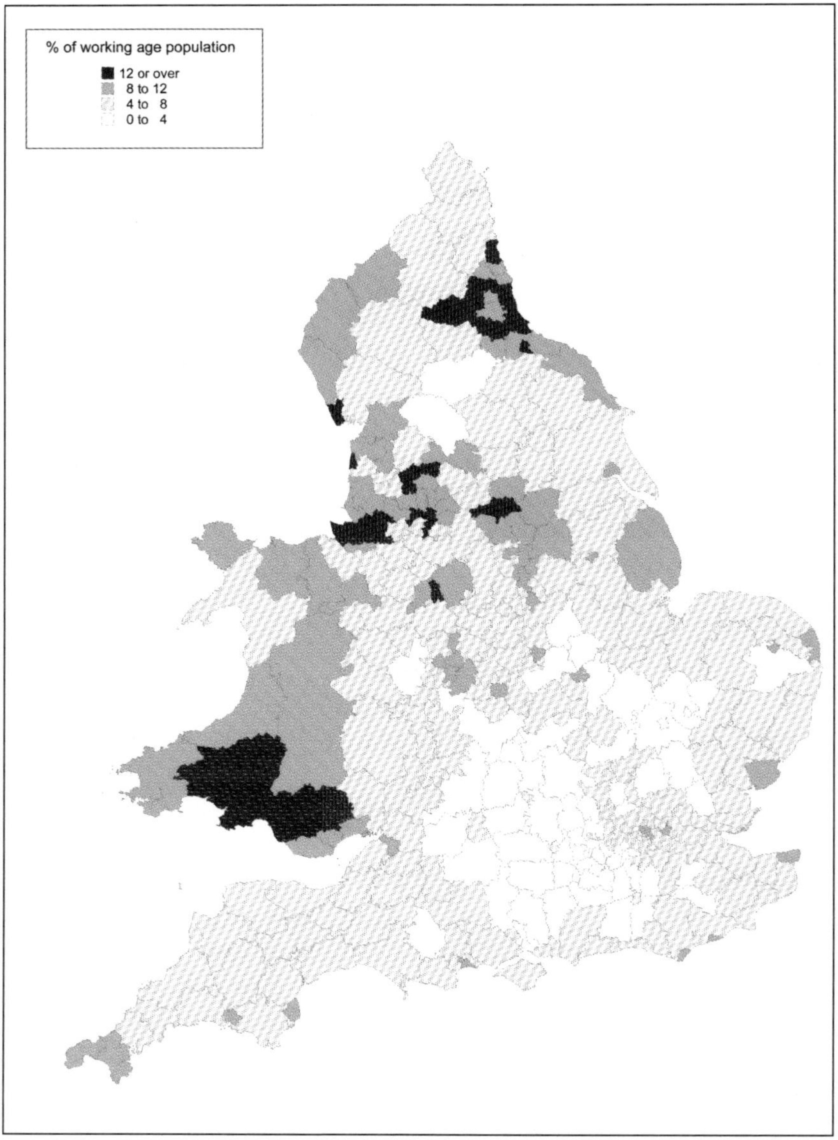

Data sources: DWP and ONS Mid-year population estimates
Digital Boundary Source: Geoplan

Figure 3: Adults of working age claiming sickness-related benefits, Scotland, August 2003

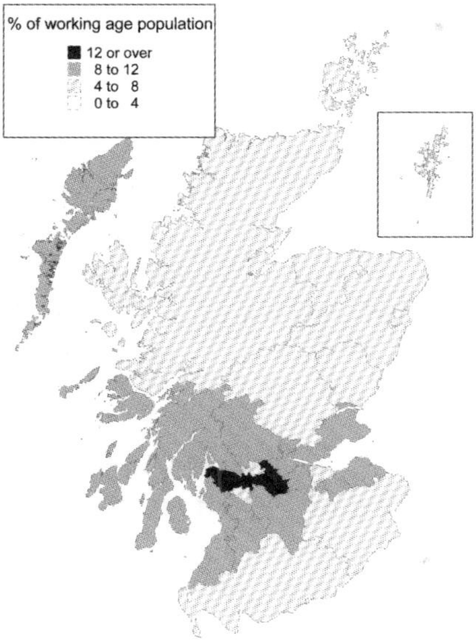

Data sources: DWP and ONS Mid-year population estimates and authors estimates
Digital Boundary Source: Geoplan

sample of claimants, which in view of the exceptionally large numbers on these benefits can be considered to provide a reliable picture. The number of claimants in each district is expressed as a percentage of the 2002 working age population, again from official data.

What is immediately apparent is that sickness claimants are especially concentrated in certain areas, notably North East England, Merseyside, South Wales, parts of Yorkshire, and Clydeside. These are the parts of Britain where industrial job losses have been concentrated over many years and where claimant unemployment has persistently been higher than the national average.

Table 1 lists the top 20 and bottom 10 districts across Britain in terms of the share of the working age population claiming sickness-related benefits. The top 20 are without exception older industrial districts in the North, Scotland and Wales. Around half are former coalmining areas and no fewer than seven cover the Welsh Valleys.

The top 20 also includes some substantial cities – Glasgow, Liverpool, Stoke and Manchester. Inner London boroughs, which often have relatively high claimant unemployment, are conspicuous by their absence from this list. At the other end of the scale, the bottom 10 are all small town and rural districts in the south and east of Britain. The difference between the extremes is considerable – there are twelve times as many sickness claimants, in relation to the local population, in Easington district in County Durham as in Hart district in Hampshire.

In Easington and in Merthyr Tydfil in the Welsh Valleys, more than one in five of all adults of working age – ie of all 16-64 year old men and all 16-59 year old women – are out of work and on sickness benefits. In Glasgow and in Liverpool the proportion is one in six. In Glasgow, 63,600 men and women of working age are on these benefits. In Liverpool the figure is 45,000. The proportions among men are still worse: in Easington and Merthyr Tydfil, 24 per cent of all working age men – just under one in four – are out of work and claiming sickness benefits. None of these men are included in the claimant unemployment figures.

Within specific segments of the workforce the incidence of sickness claimants is even greater. Men are more likely than women to be sickness claimants, but within the male workforce it is older, manual workers with few formal qualifications who are most likely to claim these benefits (see Alcock et al 2003). The likelihood of claiming sickness benefits rises sharply with age, which is consistent with the view that older workers are more likely to experience the health problems that enable them to claim Incapacity Benefit rather than Jobseeker's Allowance. In Merthyr Tydfil, admittedly an extreme case, just over half of all men aged between 50 and 64 were sickness claimants in May 2002 (Beatty and Fothergill 2002b). In Glasgow the proportion was 44 per cent, in Liverpool 38 per cent and in Manchester 36 per cent.

In total there are 68 districts in England, Scotland and Wales where in August 2003 ten per cent or more of the entire working age population was out of work and claiming sickness-related benefits. Not a single one of these districts was in London, the South East, South West or Eastern England.

Table 1 : Districts with the highest and lowest sickness claimant rates, August 2003

		% of total working age population
	Top 20	
1.	Easington	21.1
2.	Merthyr Tydfil	20.7
3.	Blaenau Gwent	19.1
4.	Neath Port Talbot	17.2
5.	Glasgow	17.2
6.	Rhondda Cynon Taff	16.7
7.	Liverpool	16.1
8.	Knowsley	16.0
9.	Caerphilly	15.6
10.	Bridgend	14.7
11.	Barrow in Furness	14.4
12.	Wear Valley	14.4
13.	Torfaen	14.4
14.	Barnsley	14.4
15.	Inverclyde	14.2
16.	North Lanarkshire	14.1
17.	Stoke on Trent	14.0
18.	Sedgefield	13.4
19.	Manchester	13.3
20.	Gateshead	13.0
	Bottom 10	
397.	Surrey Heath	2.8
398.	Wycombe	2.8
399.	Vale of White Horse	2.8
400.	Elmbridge	2.8
401.	South Northamptonshire	2.7
402.	West Berkshire	2.7
403.	Waverley	2.7
404.	South Cambridgeshire	2.7
405.	Wokingham	2.0
406	Hart	1.7

Sources: DWP and OPCS
Note : Sickness claimants refers to Incapacity Benefit (including NI credits only) and Severe Disablement Allowance

Measuring the diversion

The crucial issue is the extent to which these huge numbers represent hidden unemployment. The key analytical problem is that the headline figures for IB claimants conflate two groups – those whose health problems are so severe that they would remain on sickness benefits in all circumstances, and those who would have been in work if suitable jobs had been available. At the level of the individual, in particular, the dividing line is not easy to draw. Additionally, there are differences between areas in the underlying health of the population which mean that the number of sickness claimants is always going to vary from place to place.

Partly the problem is one of definition. In this article we set out to measure the number of sickness claimants who *could reasonably be expected to have been in work in a fully employed economy*. This is not the same as the number who are actively looking for work. Nor is it the same as the number who have actually moved directly from unemployment-related benefits (mainly JSA) to sickness-related benefits (mainly IB) since large numbers move directly from employment onto sickness benefits.

The basic approach adopted here is to establish a 'benchmark' reflecting what is achievable in a fully employed economy, and to compare actual levels in each district with that benchmark. Levels above the benchmark are deemed to represent hidden unemployment. In principle this is the method used in earlier studies (for example Beatty and Fothergill 1996) but here an improved and more robust version is deployed.

There are two components to the benchmark used here. The first is the proportion of men and women of working age who are sickness claimants in fully-employed parts of Britain. The area chosen here to represent a 'fully-employed economy' comprises the seven counties of Berkshire, Buckinghamshire, Hampshire (minus Portsmouth and Southampton), Hertfordshire, Oxfordshire, Surrey and West Sussex. These make up a block to the north, west and south of London where by 2003 there had effectively been full employment for four or five years. The share of the working-age population in work – the 'employment rate' – averaged in excess of 80 per cent in each of these counties in 2003. The employment rate in neighbouring counties to the east and south east of London (Essex, Kent, East Sussex) fell a little below this 80 per cent threshold.

In August 2003, 4.1 per cent of working age men and 3.3 per cent of working age women were sickness benefit claimants in this fully employed part of southern England. This low level illustrates what can be achieved in contemporary Britain, at least in some areas, in the context of full employment.

The second component of the benchmark is the underlying deviation in sickness levels in each district from the level in this fully employed part of southern England. Here, as a guide, we use the proportion of men and women of working age who were recorded as 'permanently sick' by the 1981 Census of Population, when the figures were still largely unaffected by the subsequent diversion into hidden unemployment[1]. This is the approach first deployed by Armstrong (1999). The excess in the proportion of 'permanently sick' in each district in 1981, over the comparable 1981 figure for the fully-employed part of the South, is added to the sickness claimant rate in the fully-employed part of the South in 2003 to give an overall benchmark for the district. The higher underlying level of incapacitating ill health in some areas is therefore built into the benchmark.

In each district the benchmark therefore takes account not only of the level of sickness claimants achievable in a fully-employed part of Britain but also of geographical variations in underlying ill-health. The benchmarking exercise has been carried out separately for men and women.

An example will make the procedure clearer. Take the case of men in Barnsley, shown in Table 2. Barnsley, a former coalmining district in South Yorkshire, has a total population of around 230,000 and a working age population of just over 130,000. In Barnsley in August 2003, 12,000 men of working age were out of work and claiming sickness-related benefits. This represented 17.4 per cent of the entire male working age population. The benchmark for Barnsley, as elsewhere, comprises two elements. First there is the sickness claimant rate among men in the fully-employed parts of the South – 4.1 per cent, equivalent to 2,800 men in the Barnsley context. Second there is the excess sickness among working age men in Barnsley, over the level in this part of the South, recorded in 1981 before the figures became badly contaminated by the diversion from unemployment – 3.4 per cent, equivalent to 2,400 men. This excess reflects the poorer underlying standard of health in Barnsley, not least as a result of employment in the coal industry. These figures give an overall benchmark of 7.5 per cent, or 5,200 men. This is the number of male sickness claimants that we would expect in Barnsley in the context of full employment. The difference between this figure and the actual number of male sickness claimants – 6,800 or 9.9 per cent of the male working age population – is what we identify as the diversion from unemployment. For comparison, the number of men who were claimant unemployed in Barnsley in August 2003 was just 2,217.

Barnsley is a fairly extreme case: it has the eleventh highest male sickness claimant rate in Britain. The point is however to illustrate the estimation process. Later we subject the resulting estimates to cross-checking by other methods, but at this point it is worth noting that the estimation procedure implicitly assumes that the underlying geography of incapacitating ill health has not changed between 1981 and 2003. In practice there will of course have been changes, but whether these will have greatly altered the relativities between districts is questionable

Table 2: The diversion from unemployment to sickness benefits: a worked example for men in Barnsley

	No. in Barnsley	*as % male working age population*
Male sickness claimants, Aug 2003	12,000	17.4
BENCHMARK		
(1) Male sickness rate in fully-employed part of South, Aug 2003	2,800	4.1
(2) Excess 'permanent sickness' in Barnsley over full-employed part of South, April 1981	2,400	3.4
Benchmark for Barnsley	5,200	7.5
Estimated diversion (Actual minus benchmark)	6,800	9.9

Sources: DWP, Census of Population

Figure 4: Hidden unemployment amongst sickness-related benefit claimants, England and Wales, August 2003

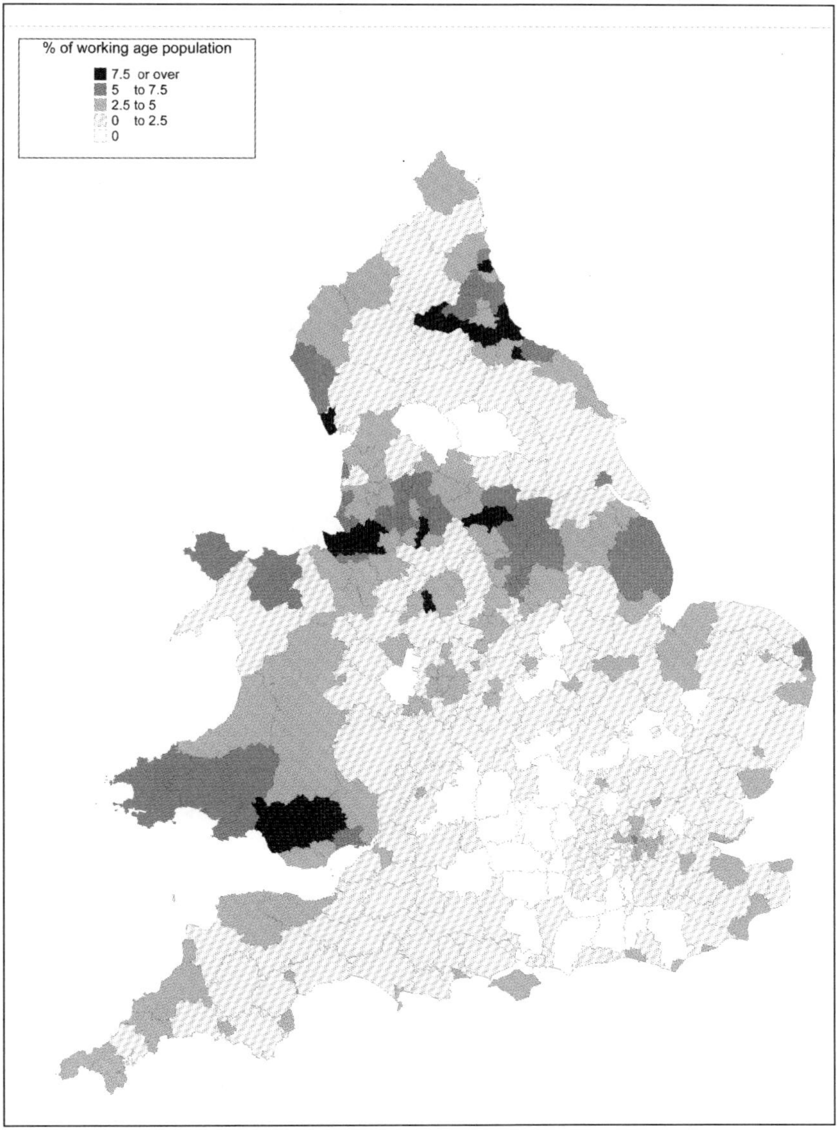

Data sources: DWP and ONS Mid-year population estimates
Digital Boundary Source: Geoplan

bearing in mind the considerable stability of socio-economic disparities at the district scale that underpin differences in standards of health. Additionally, even in 1981 there may have been limited spill-over from unemployment to sickness benefits in some districts. The figures on the diversion to sickness benefits generated by these methods therefore need to be treated as estimates. On the other hand they do attempt to take account not only of what has been shown to be achievable in fully-employed areas but also of underlying differences between districts.

New estimates of the diversion from 'unemployment' to 'sickness'
Beatty et al (2002) first applied the method outlined above to data for August 2001. Here we present new estimates for every district in Great Britain based on sickness benefit data for August 2003.

Figures 4 and 5 map the scale of estimated diversion from unemployment to sickness benefits. What the maps show is a profoundly

Figure 5: Hidden unemployment amongst sickness-related claimants, Scotland, August 2003

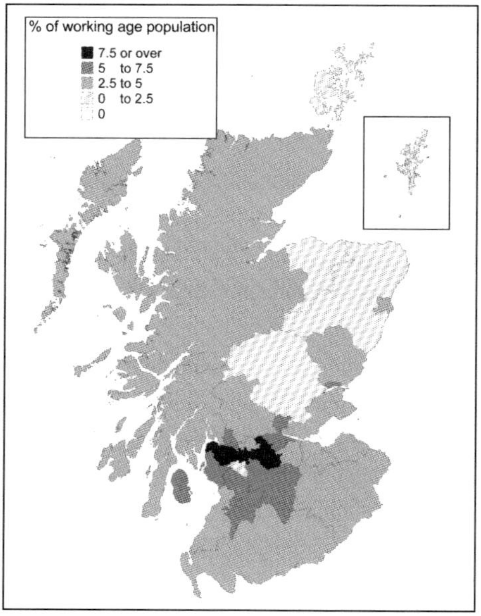

Data sources: DWP and ONS Mid-year population estimates and authors estimates
Digital Boundary Source: Geoplan

uneven distribution. At one end of the scale there are thirty districts where there is estimated to be no diversion at all. These are, in effect, the districts where full employment already prevails and there is no reason why anyone need remain on Incapacity Benefit if they want to work and are able to work. These districts are nearly all concentrated in the south and east of Britain, especially in an area to the west of London.

At the other end of the scale, there are a large number of districts in the older industrial areas of the North, Scotland and Wales where the diversion from unemployment appears to be substantial. In a handful, including Glasgow and Liverpool, the estimated diversion exceeds ten per cent of the entire adult workforce. By and large, the areas where this large diversion is estimated to occur are the same districts where the overall share of the working age population claiming sickness benefits is particularly high. In other words, even after adjusting for differences in underlying ill health these areas have large numbers of men and women who appear to have been diverted from unemployment.

Table 3 shows the regional pattern of the estimated diversion from

Table 3: Estimated diversion from unemployment to sickness benefits by region, August 2003

	No.	*as % total working age population*
North East	95,000	6.1
Wales	101,000	5.8
North West	231,000	5.6
Scotland	172,000	5.4
Yorkshire & Humber	100,000	3.3
West Midlands	107,000	3.3
East Midlands	73,000	2.8
London	103,000	2.1
South West	56,000	1.9
Eastern	47,000	1.4
South East	45,000	0.9
Great Britain	1,130,000	3.2

Source: Authors' estimates based on DWP data

unemployment to sickness benefits. This confirms the skewed regional distribution evident in the maps. In the North East, North West, Scotland and Wales, 5-6 per cent of the population of working age is estimated to have been diverted from unemployment. The proportion in the South East of England is below 1 per cent, and only 1-2 per cent in London, the South West and Eastern England. The Midlands and Yorkshire fall between the two extremes.

Table 3 also shows the numbers estimated to be part of this diversion. Across Britain as a whole it is estimated that 1,130,000 people have been diverted from unemployment to sickness benefits – 650,000 men and 470,000 women. For comparison, total claimant unemployment across Britain at the same time (August 2003) stood at just 911,000. The comparison is illuminating: it suggests that Britain has more 'hidden' unemployed among sickness claimants than 'visible' unemployed on the claimant count.

Table 4 compares these national estimates with the total numbers of sickness-related benefit claimants. This too is illuminating because it suggests that despite the enormous scale of the apparent diversion from unemployment, it accounts for only just over 40 per cent of all sickness claimants of working age. This observation holds for both men and women. In effect, what this comparison is telling us is that even if genuine full employment could be achieved in every part of the country, the total number of sickness claimants, currently rather over 2.6 million, could be expected to fall no lower than about 1.5 million.

Sickness benefit numbers around 1.5 million, even in the context of

Table 4: Estimated diversion from unemployment to sickness benefits, by sex, Great Britain, August 2003

	Total no. of sickness claimants of working age	*Estimated diversion from unemployment*	
		No.	*as % total*
Men	1,587,000	650,000	41.2
Women	1,075,000	470,000	44.2
Total	2,662,000	1,130,000	42.2

Source: Authors' estimates based on DWP data

full employment, would still represent a substantial increase on historic levels, which in the early 1980s were well below the million mark. In purely statistical terms what this reflects in our calculations is the fact that even in the fully-employed parts of the South, sickness claimant rates are now higher than they were in the early 1980s. A little of the increase through time may reflect an ageing population of working age – fewer younger workers and more over 50. The rising number of women in paid employment, who therefore accrue the NI credits that entitle them to Incapacity Benefit, may account for a little more of the increase.

More likely, changes in the workplace explain the largest part of the underlying increase in the number of sickness claimants. Whereas the numbers in physically strenuous or dangerous industries such as mining has declined, it is often argued that the pace and pressure in most workplaces has increased. Thus whereas at one time employers might have moved workers with health problems onto lighter or less demanding duties, it is questionable whether the scope for this practice now exists on anything like the same scale. The space for the less healthy worker has often gone, and sickness that was once hidden in the workplace has become visible in the benefits system.

Table 5 shows the top 20 districts in terms of the estimated share of the working age population diverted from unemployment to sickness benefits. Easington once more tops this list – one in seven of the entire working age population is estimated to fall into this category. The top 20 again includes Glasgow and Liverpool. Middlesbrough and Stoke-on-Trent also figure on the list. In these top 20 districts alone, a total of more than 210,000 people are estimated to have been diverted from unemployment to sickness benefits.

Finally, Table 6 shows the scale of the estimated diversion in each of Britain's 28 principal cities. The range varies from 11.2 per cent of the working age population in Glasgow to 1.9 per cent in Portsmouth, illustrating the point that a large-scale diversion is not something that is common to all Britain's cities. Rather, it is the former industrial cities of the North, Scotland and Wales that are estimated to have experienced the largest diversion. Although the absolute numbers in London are large, it comes third from bottom on the list in terms of share of the working age population.

Table 5: Estimated diversion from unemployment to sickness benefits, Top 20 districts, August 2003

		No.	*as % of total working age population*
1.	Easington	8,100	14.5
2.	Merthyr Tydfil	4,100	12.0
3.	Blaenau Gwent	4,700	11.3
4.	Glasgow	41,400	11.2
5.	Knowsley	9,900	10.8
6.	Neath Port Talbot	8,300	10.4
7.	Liverpool	29,000	10.4
8.	Barrow in Furness	4,300	10.1
9.	Barnsley	11,900	8.9
10.	Caerphilly	9,000	8.7
11.	Rhondda Cynon Taff	12,100	8.7
12.	North Lanarkshire	17.300	8.5
13.	Inverclyde	4,300	8.4
14.	Halton	6,200	8.4
15.	Middlesbrough	6,800	8.3
16.	Stoke on Trent	12,200	8.3
17.	Hartlepool	4,200	8.0
18.	Blyth Valley	4,100	7.9
19.	Renfrewshire	8,500	7.9
20	Bridgend	6,000	7.7

Source: Authors' estimates based on DWP data

How reliable?

The estimates of the number diverted from unemployment to sickness benefits (or more particularly the men within this group) can be cross-checked against estimates derived by four alternative methods. Two are statistical comparisons using alternative benchmarks. One uses South East sickness data for 1991, when this region had just come to the end of an earlier period of effectively full employment. This 1991 South East benchmark was the basis of earlier published estimates of hidden unemployment (for example Beatty and Fothergill 1996). The other statistical comparison uses national

Table 6: Estimated diversion from unemployment to sickness benefits, principal cities, August 2003

	No.	as % of total working age population
Glasgow	41,400	11.2
Liverpool	29,000	10.4
Middlesbrough	6,800	8.3
Stoke on Trent	12,200	8.3
Manchester	20,600	7.5
Sunderland	12,200	7.0
Swansea	9,300	6.9
Dundee	5,100	5.7
Newcastle upon Tyne	9,000	5.4
Hull	7,600	5.1
Nottingham	8,400	4.8
Birmingham	27,800	4.6
Coventry	8,300	4.4
Norwich	3,500	4.4
Plymouth	6,400	4.3
Leicester	6,900	3.9
Bradford	10,800	3.8
Bristol	9,400	3.8
Cardiff	7,200	3.7
Derby	4,900	3.6
Aberdeen	4,800	3.5
Sheffield	10,500	3.3
Edinburgh	8,400	2.8
Brighton	4,200	2.6
Southampton	3,300	2.3
London	103,000	2.1
Leeds	9,200	2.0
Portsmouth	2,300	1.9

Source : Authors' estimates based on DWP data

sickness data for 1981, before the figures became badly contaminated by the diversion from unemployment[2]. The third and fourth alternative estimates are based on survey data for male IB claimants (see Alcock et al 2003).

In Britain as a whole in August 2003 a total of 1,470,000 men of working age were claiming Incapacity Benefit. The four alternative methods generate the following estimates of hidden unemployment among this group of men across Britain as a whole:

Using the level of 'permanent sickness' in the South East in 1991 as the benchmark	680,000
Using the national (GB) level of 'permanent sickness' in 1981 as the benchmark	730,000
Using the share of male IB claimants who say they would like a full-time job (47%)	690,000
Using the share of male IB claimants who lost their last job mainly for reasons other than ill-health or injury (52%)	760,000

The number of men diverted from unemployment to sickness benefits across Britain, generated by the methods used in this article, is 650,000. The fact that five separate methods point to a diversion of between 650,000 and 760,000 gives considerable confidence. The method adopted in this paper, however, remains the one most likely to generate robust figures at the district scale because it takes account not only of what has already been shown to be possible in fully-employed areas but also of underlying geographical variations in incapacitating ill health

A further check on the reliability of the estimates comes from a comparison with Labour Force Survey data. An analysis of this information for 2001-02 (*Labour Market Trends* 2002) shows that of the 7.2 million men and women of working age in the UK who had a current work-limiting health problem or disability, 15.7 per cent or 1.13 million were economically inactive but said they would like a job. By comparison, the total number of men and women in Great Britain in August 2003 who are estimated to have been diverted from unemployment to sickness benefits using the methods in this report is identical at 1.13 million, though our methods point to around 50,000 more men and 50,000 fewer women than this comparison with LFS disability data.

There must nevertheless be a residual question mark about the estimates for women. The rising number of women claiming sickness-related benefits sits oddly alongside what is generally recognised to be a labour market that is providing growing job opportunities for women. At least part of the increase in the number of women claiming these benefits may in fact represent a diversion from other benefits (such as Income Support for lone parents) rather than from unemployment. Exactly how many of the 1.1 million women of working age on sickness benefits might have been in work in a fully employed economy is a question that really requires further research.

In what sense unemployed?

It is important to be clear about the nature of the diversion from unemployment to sickness benefits that our methods identify. These are people who might reasonably be expected to have been in work in a fully employed economy. As we noted earlier, they are not necessarily active job seekers. However, the fact that some do not actively look for work should not disqualify them for inclusion because where appropriate jobs are in short supply many people are realistic enough to know that they are unlikely to find suitable employment. They therefore give up looking for work, but that does not make them any less unemployed.

It is also important to emphasise that there is nothing fraudulent about the behaviour of the large number of people who now claim Incapacity Benefit. All these men and women will have been given the appropriate medical certification to entitle them to IB. The health limitations are genuine, even if not necessarily always fully incapacitating in all circumstances. What has happened is that job loss has fallen disproportionately on less healthy workers, many of whom are also older and less skilled. These people have then found themselves at the back of the queue for jobs. The benefits system and the employment services have then interacted to divert large numbers away from recorded unemployment and into recorded sickness.

Hidden unemployment, on Incapacity Benefit, is nevertheless different in some ways from conventional claimant unemployment. Because so many of the men and women on Incapacity Benefit have given up actively seeking work their unemployment may be less painful than for JSA claimants. They no longer have to endure failed job applications and dashed hopes. Also, because of their detachment from the labour market they do not form part of the stock of potential workers from whom employers choose and consequently they exert no downward pressure on wage inflation. Often the hidden unemployed may have become reconciled to their position outside the labour market. In a sense what has happened, after two decades in which labour markets have been slack in many parts of the country, is that unemployment has filtered down to rest with the groups who find it most difficult to hold onto jobs – older workers, the less healthy, less skilled and women with young children at home. As their status on the margins of the workforce has been consolidated, these groups have increasingly drawn on benefits other than JSA or have been denied access to benefits altogether. Their unemployment has slipped from view.

But none of this changes the fact that very large numbers of those who now claim sickness-related benefits, above all Incapacity Benefit, could have been expected to be in work in a genuinely fully employed economy. Indeed, the much smaller number of sickness claimants prior to the 1980s and 90s indicates that far more people with health problems were once in employment.

Perceptions of the British labour market

The analysis presented in this paper represents a challenge to the way that the contemporary British labour market is perceived. The conventional view, largely rooted in claimant unemployment data, is that the economy is close to full employment with residual joblessness on only a modest scale in some parts of the country.

There is nothing in the evidence presented here that contradicts the view that the British labour market has improved a great deal during the long period of continuous economic growth from around 1993 onwards. This has cut the number of claimant unemployed by around two-thirds. However, the figures presented here show that economic growth has had no discernible impact on the number of jobless people claiming sickness benefits. The men and women on these benefits now constitute by far the largest group of working-age claimants. Furthermore, our analysis indicates that more than a million of the men and women claiming sickness benefits have been diverted from unemployment. In other word, the true extent of unemployment is much greater than official figures indicate.

Labour ministers are therefore entirely correct in arguing that too many people have become 'parked' on Incapacity Benefit. However, what the same ministers have failed to acknowledge is the extent to which this now hides the real level of unemployment.

The other important conclusion from our analysis is that the regional imbalances in British labour markets are far more severe than has generally been recognised, and certainly far worse than claimant unemployment figures suggest. The problem is not simply that large numbers have been diverted from unemployment to sickness benefits but that this diversion has happened predominantly in the older industrial areas of the North, Scotland and Wales. These areas not only have above average claimant unemployment (which is recognised already) but also exceptionally large numbers who have been diverted from unemployment to sickness benefits. In contrast there are substantial parts of the South of England where, even after taking account of the diversion onto sickness benefits, full employment (or something close to it) genuinely does appear to exist.

It is undoubtedly true that many of the men on Incapacity Benefit are the workers who were displaced during the last two decades from industries such as coal, steel and heavy engineering, and that many of these men are now in their fifties and early sixties. As they reach state pension they will move off IB. Crucially, however, when this marginalized cohort finally reaches retirement age they will not free up jobs for the generations behind them, including the young people continuing to enter the workforce each year. What this means for many areas is that the present imbalance in the labour market is likely to be perpetuated. Only job creation (on the labour demand side) or out-migration and out-commuting (on the labour supply side) would restore the balance that is currently missing. Furthermore, there is the real prospect that with tighter rules now controlling access to Incapacity Benefit more of the continuing imbalances in weaker local labour markets will eventually begin to show up as claimant unemployment. In other words, the extensive local joblessness identified by our figures will not just fade away as the large groups of ex-miners, ex-steelworkers and others finally reach pension age.

Implications for policy

The UK government is well aware of the need to bring down the very large numbers claiming Incapacity Benefit in order to boost labour supply, raise the capacity of the economy and cut the benefits bill. Its current approach is a variant of the policies deployed in New Deal programmes for the claimant unemployed. The emphasis is on the individual – on providing advice and training, re-motivation and the removal of financial disincentives to return to work. In the case of IB claimants, the measures are backed up by the intention to introduce more regular medical assessments.

It is hard to be critical of advice and practical support when it is generally welcome to those who benefit from it. On the other hand, the government's approach to Incapacity Benefit claimants can be criticised because the resources made available to date fall far short of those devoted to unemployed JSA claimants. As a result, the employment services have so far barely scratched the surface of the Incapacity Benefit problem, with few claimants benefiting from the emerging initiatives.

A more serious criticism, supported by the data presented here, is that the starting point of the government's efforts is simply wrong. The initiatives implicitly assume that this is a *labour supply* problem. The marked concentration in Britain's older industrial areas, on the other hand, suggests that in fact it is a *labour demand* issue. Very large numbers have been diverted from unemployment to sickness benefits in these areas because there have not been enough suitable jobs in these places. Indeed, the rising numbers on Incapacity Benefit in these areas represents the principal labour market response to job destruction in the 1980s and 1990s.

The counter-argument to this criticism is that even if job destruction was the ultimate cause of the large-scale shift onto Incapacity Benefit, these marginalized workers will not be re-engaged with the labour market without significant supply-side intervention. There is probably some truth in this. In practice, substantial numbers of older men on Incapacity Benefit will probably not now be re-engaged with the labour market in any circumstances. Their marginalization has become entrenched by years without work and they can just about get by on a combination of IB, other top-up benefits, perhaps a small pension from a former employer and possibly a spouse's income as well. Some still harbour vague aspirations to work, but others have given up entirely and now see themselves as retired. In this sense Incapacity Benefit acts as a bridge to state pension.

The trouble is that labour supply measures are most relevant where there is a strong demand for labour. Putting aside certain skills that are in short supply everywhere, in the UK context the areas where there is unquestionably a strong demand for labour are mostly in the South of England. Yet it is in the South that the diversion from unemployment to sickness benefits appears to be modest at best. There therefore seems to be only limited scope for boosting labour supply in the South through targeting IB claimants, though if IB claimants there can be re-engaged with the labour market they are likely to find a ready demand for their skills.

The much larger problem in the older industrial areas of the North requires a different approach. Fundamentally, labour demand in these regions needs to be boosted. This has happened as a result of national economic growth over the last ten years but, as we explained the main effect has been to reduce claimant unemployment leaving the stock of IB claimants largely untouched. Unfortunately, further macroeconomic stimulus to growth, for example through lower interest rates, would now run up against the constraint of an already tight labour market in large parts of southern England. This in turn would risk fuelling inflation.

There is an inexorable logic here that points to regional economic policy as the way forward. The pressing need is for policies that divert incremental demand for labour to the parts of the country where there remains substantial labour market slack among the claimant unemployed but more particularly among the very large numbers diverted onto sickness benefits. Indeed, with full employment in parts of the South, regional economic policy is arguably now the essential tool to achieve the government's stated goal of full employment.

The rhetoric emerging from Britain's Labour government is in this respect sending all the right messages. Regional policy is higher on the agenda than for more than two decades. However, whether the aspirations are yet matched by practical policies that can really deliver economic convergence between the UK regions still remains in doubt.

Notes

1 In a small number of mainly rural districts the data on permanent sickness in 1981 is inflated by the location of large psychiatric institutions, which have virtually all subsequently closed. To adjust for this potential distortion, in the districts where according to the 1981 Census of Population the proportion of the working age population living in such institutions exceeded one per cent, the excess is deducted from the 1981 permanent sickness data for that district.

2 Both statistical comparisons deduct short-term (ie less than six months) IB claimants from the headline figure to improve comparability with Census 'permanent sickness' data.

Literature

Alcock, P., Beatty, C., Fothergill, S., Macmillan, R. and Yeandle, S. (2003) *Work to Welfare: how men become detached from the labour market*, CUP, Cambridge.

Armstrong, D. (1999) 'Hidden male unemployment in Northern Ireland', *Regional Studies*, vol 33, pp 499-512.

Bartley, M. and Owen, C. (1996) 'Relation between socio-economic status, employment and health during economic change, 1973-93', *British Medical Journal*, vol 13, pp 445-49.

Beatty, C. and Fothergill, S. (1996) 'Labour market adjustment in areas of chronic industrial decline: the case of the UK coalfields', *Regional Studies*, vol 30, pp 627-40.

Beatty, C. and Fothergill, S. (1997) *Unemployment and the Labour Market in Rural Development Areas*, Rural Research Series no. 30, Rural Development Commission, London.

Beatty, C. and Fothergill, S. (2002a) 'Hidden unemployment among men: a case study', *Regional Studies*, vol 36, pp 811-823.

Beatty, C. and Fothergill, S. (2002b) *Moving Older People into Jobs: Jobcentre Plus, New Deal and the job shortfall for the over 50s*, Third Age Employment Network, London.

Beatty, C. and Fothergill, S. (2003) *The Seaside Economy*, CRESR, Sheffield Hallam University, Sheffield.

Beatty, C., Fothergill, S., Gore, T. and Green, A. (2002) *The Real Level of Unemployment 2002*, CRESR, Sheffield Hallam University, Sheffield.

Beatty, C., Fothergill, S. and Macmillan, R. (2000) 'A theory of employment, unemployment and sickness', *Regional Studies*, vol 34, pp 617-30.

Bellaby, P. and Bellaby, F. (1999) 'Unemployment and ill-health: local labour markets and ill-health in Britain 1984-91', *Work, Employment and Society*, vol 13, 461-82.

Convery, P. (1996) 'How many people are unemployed?', *Working Brief*, no 78, pp 23-26.

Easterlow, D. and Smith, S. (2003) 'Health and employment: towards a New Deal', *Policy and Politics*, vol 31, pp 511-33.

Fieldhouse, E. and Hollywood, E. (1999) 'Life after mining: hidden unemployment and changing patterns of economic activity among miners in England and Wales 1981-91', *Work, Employment and Society*, vol 13, 483-502.

Green, A. E. (1997) 'Exclusion, unemployment and non-employment', *Regional Studies*, vol 31, pp 505-20.

Green, A. E. (1999) 'Insights into unemployment and non-employment in Europe using alternative measures', *Regional Studies*, vol 33, pp 453-64.

Green, A. E. and Owen, D. (1998) *Where are the Jobless?: changing unemployment and non-employment in cities and regions*, Policy Press, Bristol.

Gregg, P. (1994) 'Out for the count: a social scientist's account of unemployment statistics in the UK', *Journal of the Royal Statistical Society A*, vol 157, pp 253-70.

Gregg, P. and Wadsworth, J. (1998) *Unemployment and non-employment: unpacking economic inactivity*, Economic Report no 12, Employment Policy Institute, London.

Labour Market Trends (2002) vol 110, p. 298.

MacKay, R. (1999) 'Work and nonwork: a more difficult labour market', *Environment and Planning A*, vol 31, pp 487-502.

Royal Statistical Society (1995) *Report of the Working Party on the Measurement of Unemployment in the UK*, Royal Statistical Society, London.

Sutherland, J. (1999) ' Further reflections on hidden unemployment: an examination of the off-flows from the claimant count in the North West of England', *Regional Studies*, vol 33, pp 456-76.

Turok, I. and Edge, N. (1999) *The Jobs Gap in Britain's Cities*, Policy Press, Bristol.

Also available from Socialist Renewal

Workers' Control
Another World is Possible
by Ken Coates price £7.99

Opening and Innovation
by Partito Rifondazione Comunista price £2

Physician, Heal Thyself
The NHS Needs a Voice of Its Own
by Duncan Smith price £2

Railtracks in the Sky
'New' Labour, Air Transport Deregulation and the Competitive Market
by Peter Reed price £9.99

New Labour's US-Style Executive Mayors
The Private Contractors' Panacea
by Peter Latham price £2

The Third Way ... or Feeding the Fat Cats
by Michael Barratt Brown price £2

The Flame, Not the Ashes
by Lionel Jospin price £2

Straw Wars: Full Spectrum Sycophancy
Jack Straw's Briefing on Missile Defence
with a response by Ken Coates price £3

Public Services or Private Profit
by Dexter Whitfield price £2

The Captive Local State
by Peter Latham price £2

Safety First?: Did the Health and Safety Commission Do Its Job?
by Christopher Gifford price £2

Third Way ... Where to?
An exchange between Tony Blair, Ken Coates and Michael Barratt Brown price £2

Towards a More Equal Society
by David Donnison price £2

The Captive Party: How Labour Was Taken over by Capital
by Michael Barratt Brown price £5

Welfare Reform: Means-tested versus Universal Benefits
by John Grieve Smith price £2

Subscription details available on request